A STREETCAR NAMED DESIRE

BY
TENNESSEE WILLIAMS

★

★

DRAMATISTS
PLAY SERVICE
INC.

NOTE ON BILLING

Anyone receiving permission to produce A STREETCAR NAMED DESIRE is required to give credit to the Author as sole and exclusive Author of the Play on the title page of all programs distributed in connection with performances of the Play and in all instances in which the title of the Play appears, including printed or digital materials for advertising, publicizing or otherwise exploiting the Play and/or a production thereof. Please see your production license for font size and typeface requirements.

Be advised that there may be additional credits required in all programs and promotional material. Such language will be listed under the "Additional Billing" section of production licenses. It is the licensee's responsibility to ensure any and all required billing is included in the requisite places, per the terms of the license.

A STREETCAR NAMED DESIRE is presented by arrangement with Dramatists Play Service, Inc. on behalf of The University of the South, Sewanee, Tennessee.

ALL TENNESSEE WILLIAMS PLAYS

The Play must be performed as published in the DPS authorized edition. It is understood that there will be no nudity in the Play unless specifically indicated in the script and that nothing in the stage presentation or stage business will alter the spirit of the Play as written.

A STREETCAR NAMED DESIRE was first produced by Irene Selznick at the Barrymore Theatre in New York City on December 3, 1947. It was directed by Elia Kazan, and the setting and lighting were by Joe Mielziner. The cast was as follows:

NEGRO WOMAN .... Gee Gee James
EUNICE HUBBELL .... Peg Hillias
STANLEY KOWALSKI ....,,,,..............,,,,,,....... Marlon Brando
STELLA KOWALSKI .... Kim Hunter
STEVE HUBBELL .... Rudy Bond
HAROLD MITCHELL (Mitch) .... Karl Malden
MEXICAN WOMAN .... Edna Thomas
BLANCHE DUBOIS .... Jessica Tandy
PABLO GONZALES ,... Nick Dennis
A YOUNG COLLECTOR .... Vito Christi
STRANGE WOMAN (Nurse) .... Ann Dere
STRANGE MAN (Doctor) .... Richard Garrick
A few nonspeaking parts, a sailor, supernumeraries, etc.

The scene is the two rooms of the Kowalski apartment in the French Quarter of New Orleans. The action of the play takes place in the spring, summer and early fall.

A STREETCAR NAMED DESIRE

ACT I

SCENE 1

Curtain rises in darkness. Music of a small jazz band is heard off. Lights come up slowly, revealing the two rooms of the Kowalski apartment in the French Quarter of New Orleans.

In the bedroom at L., *Stella Kowalski lounges in a rickety armchair, fanning herself with a palm-leaf fan and eating chocolates from a paper bag. She is reading a movie magazine.*

To her L. *two steps* lead up to a closed door that leads to bathroom. Above bathroom, in upper* L. *corner, curtained doorway gives upon a closet. Living room,* R. *of* C., *is empty. There is an imaginary wall between the two rooms, and upstage, near* C., *a draw-curtain is suspended beneath a broken fan-light in "arch" above doorway that joins the rooms.* U. R., *in living room, a low door opens upon a roofless porch. Just to* R. *of door, a spiral staircase leads to an apartment above.*

On stair are seated two persons, a languid Negro woman, who fans herself with a palm-leaf fan, and Eunice Hubbell, occupant of the apartment above, who is eating peanuts and reading a "confession" magazine. To R. *of spiral stair and porch, an alleyway leads up to level of street, which runs across stage behind the two rooms of the Kowalski apartment, and can be seen, when lighted, through back walls of apartment, these being constructed of gauze on which the outlines of windows*

---

* These may be omitted: not essential.

are appliquéd. Beyond drop that falls immediately behind the street—this drop also being of gauze—one can see a back-drop suggesting railroad tracks, which pass close by.

AT RISE: *A woman carrying a shopping-bag full of parcels passes wearily across the stage from D. R. to U. L.—and out. From U. L., behind gauze wall of apartment, Stanley Kowalski enters, followed by Harold Mitchell—Mitch—his friend. Stanley hurries along street R. toward door of his apartment. Mitch lopes along behind Stanley, trying to keep up with the former's stride. Music is still heard. Lights have grown brighter.*

STANLEY. *(Opening his door, bellowing into living room.)* Hey, Stella! Hey, there, Stella, baby!

> *The Negro woman smiles big. Mitch waits D. R. for Stanley. Stella jumps up from armchair, comes into living room.*

STELLA. Don't holler at me like that.

STANLEY. *(Tossing package of meat covered with blood to Stella.)* Catch!

STELLA. *(Catching package.)* What?

STANLEY. Meat!

> *Stanley and Mitch start out D. R.*

STELLA. *(Running to front door with package.)* Stanley! Where are you going?

STANLEY. *(Off.)* Bowling!

STELLA. *(Leaning out door, calling.)* Can I come watch?

STANLEY. *(Farther off.)* Come on!

STELLA. Be over soon! *(Patting Eunice's shoulder.)* Hello, Eunice. How are you?

EUNICE. I'm all right.

> *Stella puts meat package on table in living room, takes look at herself in a mirror tacked inside door of a low cabinet, which is upstage between an icebox and a daybed along back wall of living room. Eunice leans forward, calls after Stella.*

Tell Steve to get him a poor boy's sandwich, 'cause nothing's left here.

Stella steps over a broom lying on floor just inside front door, and comes out onto porch, closing apartment door behind her. She hurries out D. R. Eunice and the Negro woman laugh.

NEGRO WOMAN. *(Nudges Eunice with her elbow.)* What was that package he threw at her? *(Laughs.)*

EUNICE. *(Amused.)* You hush now!

NEGRO WOMAN. *(Imitating Stanley's gesture of throwing meat.)* Catch what!

The women laugh together.

Blanche DuBois enters from U. L. and comes along street behind gauze wall. She is carrying a small suitcase in one hand and a slip of paper in the other. As she looks about, her expression is one of shocked disbelief. Her appearance is incongruous to the setting. She looks as if she were arriving at a summer tea or cocktail party in the garden district. She is about five years older than Stella. There is something about her uncertain manner that suggests a moth.

A sailor, in whites, enters from U. R., and approaches Blanche. He asks her a question, which is not heard because of the music. She looks bewildered, and cannot, apparently, answer him. He passes on and out U. L. Music fades away. Blanche comes around corner at R. and approaches the women on spiral stair. Lights in street commence to dim, and interior lighting in apartment brightens. Eunice looks at Blanche—then at Negro woman, back at Blanche.

EUNICE. *(To Blanche.)* What's the matter, honey? Are you lost?

BLANCHE. *(Speaking with a faintly hysterical humor.)* They told me to take a streetcar named Desire, transfer to one called Cemetery, and ride six blocks and get off at Elysian Fields!

EUNICE. That's where you are at now.

BLANCHE. At Elysian Fields?

EUNICE. This here is Elysian Fields.

Negro woman laughs.

BLANCHE. They mustn't have—understood—what number I wanted...

EUNICE. What number you lookin' for?

BLANCHE. *(Refers wearily to slip of paper in hand.)* Six thirty-two.

EUNICE. *(Indicating number "632" beside door of apartment.)* You don't have to look no further.

Negro woman laughs.

BLANCHE. *(Uncomprehendingly.)* I'm looking for my sister, Stella DuBois—I mean—Mrs. Stanley Kowalski.

Negro woman nudges Eunice, yawns broadly.

EUNICE. That's the party. You just did miss her, though.

Negro woman rises, stretches, moves a step D. R.

BLANCHE. This? Can this be her home?

EUNICE. She's got the downstairs and I've got the up.

BLANCHE. Oh. She's out?

EUNICE. *(Pointing off D. R.)* You noticed that bowling alley around the corner?

BLANCHE. I'm—not sure I did.

EUNICE. Well, that's where she's at—watchin' her husband bowl.

Negro woman laughs.

You want to leave your suitcase here an' go find her?

BLANCHE. *(Moving downstage on porch.)* No...

NEGRO WOMAN. I'll go tell her she come.

BLANCHE. *(Putting down suitcase.)* Thanks.

Negro woman yawns, stretches, fanning herself, slouches out D. R., drawling a "Yo' welcome" to Blanche's "Thank you."

EUNICE. *(Rising.)* She wasn't expecting you?

BLANCHE. *(Crumpling slip of paper, throwing it away.)* No. No, not tonight.

Eunice puts bag of peanuts in dress pocket.

EUNICE. Well, why don't you just go in and make yourself at home till they get back?

BLANCHE. How could I do that?

EUNICE. *(Coming down step.)* We own this place, so I can let you in.

Eunice slaps front door with flat of her palm, and it flies open. Blanche enters living room, stands with some trepidation just above table. Takes in the room. Eunice looks at Blanche, then at her suitcase, then picks up Blanche's suitcase, steps into room, sets suitcase beside kitchen cabinet, picks up broom from floor near door. Puts broom against R. side of icebox, then notices Blanche's expression. Eunice moves to pick up two of Stella's dresses which have been lying on daybed, and starts toward bedroom with them. She has closed front door.

(As she picks up broom.) It's kinda messed up right now, but when it's clean it's real sweet.

BLANCHE. *(Looking about.)* Is it?

EUNICE. Uh-huh, I think so. So you're Stella's sister?

BLANCHE. *(Lifting her veil.)* Yes. *(Wanting to get rid of Eunice.)* Thanks for letting me in.

EUNICE. *(In bedroom, spreading or brushing bed a bit.)* Por nada, as the Mexicans say—por nada! Stella spoke of you.

She disposes of dresses in bedroom on bed and on her way back picks up apple from a small dish on radio table just inside bedroom door.

BLANCHE. *(Takes off gloves.)* Yes?

EUNICE. I think she said you taught school. *(Has returned, stands C.)*

BLANCHE. Yes.

EUNICE. *(At L-shaped bench in living room; faces Blanche.)* And you're from Mississippi, huh? *(Wipes apple on sleeve of dress.)*

BLANCHE. Yes.

EUNICE. She showed me a picture of your home place, the plantation. *(Sits.)*

BLANCHE. Belle Reve?

EUNICE. A great big place with white columns. *(Bites into apple.)*

BLANCHE. —Yes…

EUNICE. Sure must be a job to keep up, a place like that.

BLANCHE. If you will excuse me, I'm just about to drop.

EUNICE. Sure, honey. Why don't you set down? *(Eats apple.)*

9

BLANCHE. What I meant was I'd like to be left alone.

Eunice, apple at mouth—pauses—pats foot—rises. Offended, she starts above Blanche toward front door R.

EUNICE. Well, I don't need a wall of bricks to fall on me!

BLANCHE. I didn't mean to be rude, but—

EUNICE. *(Patting Blanche on the arm.)* I'll just drop by the bowling alley and hustle her up.

Eunice goes out, closing door, exits D. R. Blanche looks about her. Takes a few uncertain steps toward bedroom, looks in. Turns back, spies open door of kitchen cabinet, crosses to it, removes a whiskey bottle and glass. Comes to above table, pours herself stiff drink. Puts down glass. Then picks it up again, shakes out last drops of liquor onto carpet, and takes glass and bottle back to cabinet. Moves uncertainly to the L-shaped seat, sits. A cat screams off R. Blanche, frightened, leaps up.

BLANCHE. I've got to keep hold of myself.

Stella hurries on from D. R., followed by Eunice, and rushes into apartment. Eunice goes up spiral stairs to her apartment.

STELLA. *(Calling out joyfully as she opens door.)* Blanche! Blanche!

For a moment, the sisters stare at one another. Stella darts to a light switch in U. R. corner of living room, beneath spiral stair, touches switch and floods room with light. Then rushes into her sister's arms.

BLANCHE. Stella, oh Stella, Stella! Stella for Star!

Her following speeches are delivered with a feverish vivacity, as if she feared for either of them to stop and think.

Now, then, let me look at you. *(Turns away.)* But don't you look at me, Stella, no, no, no, not till later, not till I've bathed and rested! And turn that over-light off! Turn that off! I won't be looked at in this merciless glare!

Stella laughs and complies, going to U. R. switch. The harsh light snaps off.

Come back here, now! Oh, my baby! Stella! Stella for Star!

She embraces Stella again.

I thought you would never come back to this horrible place! What am I saying? I didn't mean to say that. I meant to be nice about it and say—oh, what a convenient location and such—Precious lamb, you haven't said a word to me.

STELLA. You haven't given me a chance to, honey.

She laughs, embraces Blanche, but her glance at her sister is a little anxious.

BLANCHE. Well, now, you talk. Open your pretty mouth and talk while I look around for some liquor. *(Crosses above Stella to R., by table.)* I know you must have some liquor on the place. Where can it be, I wonder? *(Turns upstage.)* Oh, I spy! I spy!

Blanche crosses to kitchen cabinet, takes bottle and glass from it. They nearly slip from her grasp. She is shaking, panting for breath, and tries to laugh. Stella moves to L. of Blanche, takes bottle.

STELLA. Blanche, you sit down and let me pour the drinks.

Blanche retreats to C. of living room, Stella brings bottle and glass to table R.

(Pouring a shot.) I don't know what we've got to mix with. Maybe a Coke's in the icebox.

BLANCHE. *(Seizing glass from Stella.)* No Coke, honey. Not with my nerves tonight.

Stella puts bottle on table, puts the stopper in it. Blanche crosses C. with her drink as Stella goes to icebox, opens it, and peers inside.

(Below couch.) Where—where is—?

STELLA. *(At icebox.)* Stanley? Bowling! He loves it.

Blanche drinks.

They're having a— *(Grabs bottle in icebox.)* —found some soda!— tournament!

BLANCHE. Just water, baby, to chase it.

Stella returns to table with Coke, jar of water, bottle-opener which she has picked up from top of icebox.

Now, don't get worried. Your sister hasn't turned into a drunkard.

She's just all shaken up and hot and tired and dirty. *(Crosses a bit L.)* You sit down and explain this place to me. What on earth are you doing in a place like this?

> *Stella puts water jar on table. Sits in chair above table, opens Coke, sips it.*

STELLA. Now, Blanche.

BLANCHE. Oh, I'm not going to be hypocritical. I'm going to be honestly critical. *(Crosses L., looks into bedroom.)* Never, never, never in my worst dreams could I picture— *(Turning back to Stella.)* Only Poe! Only Mr. Edgar Allan Poe—could do it justice! *(Gestures toward street.)* Out there, I suppose, is the ghoul-haunted woodland of Weir! *(Laughs.)*

STELLA. No, honey—those are the L&N tracks.

BLANCHE. *(Taking step toward Stella.)* No, now seriously, putting joking aside. Why didn't you tell me? Why didn't you write me? Honey, why didn't you let me know? *(A step nearer.)*

STELLA. Tell you what, Blanche?

BLANCHE. Why, that you had to live in these conditions?

> *Stella rises, putting down Coke, crosses to Blanche.*

STELLA. Aren't you being a little intense about it? It's not that bad at all! New Orleans isn't like other cities. *(Puts hands gently on Blanche.)*

BLANCHE. *(Moving from Stella's touch.)* This has got nothing to do with New Orleans. You might as well say— *(Pats Stella.)* —forgive me, blessed baby. The subject is closed. *(Moves D. R. one step.)*

STELLA. *(Starting L., above Blanche.)* Thanks.

BLANCHE. *(Restraining Stella with her voice.)* You're all I've got in the world, and you're not glad to see me! *(Looks into her shaking glass, then crosses to L. of table.)*

STELLA. *(Moving to Blanche's L., takes her.)* Why, Blanche, you know that's not true.

BLANCHE. *(Turns to her.)* NO?—I'd forgotten how quiet you are.

STELLA. *(Crossing into bedroom.)* You never did give me a chance to say much, honey.

Stella picks up fan, magazine and candy from armchair, takes them to chest near closet door U. L.

So I just got in the habit of being quiet around you.

BLANCHE. That's a good habit to get into.

She takes another sip from drink. Crosses C.

You haven't asked me yet how I happened to get away from the school before the spring term ended.

Stella picks up garments from bed.

STELLA. Well, I thought you'd volunteer that information if you wanted to tell me. *(Crosses into closet with garments.)*

Blanche brings drink into bedroom, pauses above armchair.

BLANCHE. You thought I'd been fired?

Stella reappears. Pulls backless chair a bit D. L. of armchair.

STELLA. No. I—thought you might have resigned…

She sits on backless chair, faces Blanche.

BLANCHE. *(Sitting on L. arm of armchair.)* I was so exhausted by all I'd been through my—nerves just broke. I was on the verge of—lunacy, almost! So Mr. Graves—Mr. Graves is the high school superintendent—he suggested I take a leave of absence.—I couldn't put all of those details into the wire… *(Drinks quickly.)* Oh, this buzzes right through me and feels so *good!*

STELLA. Won't you have another?

BLANCHE. No, one's my limit.

Blanche rises, crosses to dressing table against L. wall of bedroom. She puts her glass on dressing table, then stands above it, facing Stella.

STELLA. Sure?

Blanche looks in mirror above dressing table, turns to Stella.

BLANCHE. You haven't said a word about my appearance.

Blanche takes off hat, takes it up to bureau, and returns.

STELLA. You look just fine.

Blanche removes hat and gloves, puts them on dressing table. Keeps purse on L. arm.

13

BLANCHE. God love you for a liar! Daylight never exposed so total a ruin! But you—you've put on some weight, yes, you're just as plump as a little partridge!

She regards Stella, sitting opposite on backless chair.

And it's so becoming to you!

STELLA. Now, Blanche—

BLANCHE. *(Crossing D. L.)* Yes, it is, it is, or I wouldn't say it! You just have to watch a little around the hips.—Stand up.

STELLA. Not now.

BLANCHE. You hear me? I said stand up!

She pulls Stella to her feet. Fusses with her.

You messy child, you, you've spilt something on that pretty white lace collar! About your hair—you ought to have it cut in a feather bob with your dainty features!

She looks at Stella's hands.

Stella, you have a maid, don't you?

STELLA. *(Drifts U. C. to below bed, indicating apartment.)* No. With only two rooms it's—

BLANCHE. What? *(Crosses to L. of Stella.)* Two rooms, did you say?

STELLA. Yes, this one and—

She is embarrassed. Gestures toward living room.

BLANCHE. *(Steps toward living room.)* And the other one?

Blanche spies bottle on living room table, crosses quickly to kitchen cabinet for a fresh glass. Stella follows.

I'm going to take just one tiny little nip more, just to put the stopper on, so to speak...

She pours a drink.

Then put the bottle away. Put the bottle away! So I won't be tempted.

She drinks, extends bottle to Stella, who takes it, puts it back into cabinet. Blanche drinks, puts down glass. Stella crosses to above table. Blanche puts purse on table. Taking off her jacket, she whirls L.

I want you to take a look at *my* figure! I haven't put on one ounce in ten years. I weigh now what I weighed the summer you left Belle Reve. The summer Dad died and you left us.

She starts drifting U. C.

STELLA. *(Speaks a little wearily.)* It's just incredible, Blanche, how well you're looking.

BLANCHE. *(Touching her forehead shakily.)* Stella, there's—only two rooms? I don't see where you're going to put me.

STELLA. *(Coming to below couch in living room.)* We're going to put you right here. *(Indicates daybed.)*

BLANCHE. *(Coming to daybed, punching it.)* What kind of bed's this?—one of those collapsible things?

STELLA. Does it feel all right?

BLANCHE. *(Dubiously.)* Wonderful, honey. I don't like a bed that gives much.

She crosses into arch between rooms. Stella lies on bed.

But there's no door between the rooms, and Stanley—will it be decent? *(Turns toward Stella.)*

STELLA. Stanley is Polish, you know.

BLANCHE. Oh, yes. That's something like Irish, isn't it? *(Crosses in L., then returns.)*

STELLA. Well—

Both laugh.

BLANCHE. I brought some nice clothes to meet all your lovely friends in.

STELLA. I'm afraid you won't think they are lovely.

BLANCHE. What are they like?

STELLA. They're Stanley's friends.

BLANCHE. Polacks?

STELLA. They're a mixed lot.

BLANCHE. Heterogeneous—types?

STELLA. Oh, yes. Yes, types is right!

BLANCHE. *(C. at L. of pillar.)* Well—anyhow—I brought some nice clothes, and I'll wear them. I guess you're hoping I'll say I'll put up at a hotel, but I'm not going to put up at a hotel. I want to be *near* you, Stella; I've got to be *with* people, I *can't* be alone! Because— as you must have noticed—I'm—*not* very *well!*

> *Her voice drops, her look is frightened. Stella rises. Crosses to* R. *of Blanche, places hand on her shoulder.*

STELLA. You seem a little bit nervous or overwrought or something.

BLANCHE. Will Stanley like me, or will I be just a visiting in-law? I couldn't stand that, Stella.

STELLA. You'll get along fine together, if you'll just try not to—well— compare him with men we went out with at home.

BLANCHE. Is he so—different?

STELLA. Yes. A different species.

BLANCHE. In what way; what's he like?

STELLA. Oh, you can't describe someone you're in love with.

> *She crosses above Blanche to dressing table, picks up photo of Stanley, which, in a small frame, has a place of honor on table. Blanche crosses to above armchair, and when Stella turns to Blanche with photo, she sits in chair, facing upstage.*

Here's a picture of him!

BLANCHE. *(Taking photo.)* An officer?

STELLA. A Master Sergeant in the Engineers' Corps. Those are decorations!

BLANCHE. He must have had those on when you met him?

STELLA. I assure you I wasn't just blinded by all the brass. But of course there were things to adjust myself to later on.

BLANCHE. Such as his civilian background! How did he take it when you told him I was coming?

STELLA. Oh, Stanley doesn't know yet.

BLANCHE. *(Frightened.)* You—haven't told him?

STELLA. He's on the road a good deal.

BLANCHE. Oh. He travels?

STELLA. Yes.

BLANCHE. Good! I mean—isn't it?

STELLA. *(Takes photo.)* I can hardly stand it when he's away for a night...

BLANCHE. Why, Stella!

STELLA. When he's away for a week, I nearly go wild!

BLANCHE. *(Crossing u. l.)* Gracious!

STELLA. And when he comes back I cry on his lap like a baby. *(Drops head to elbow on back of armchair.)*

BLANCHE. *(Crossing to head of bed.)* I guess that is what is meant by being in love...

> Stella looks up with a radiant smile.

Stella—

STELLA. What?

BLANCHE. *(In an uneasy rush.)* I haven't asked you the things you probably thought I was going to ask you. So I expect you to be understanding about what *I* have to tell *you.*

STELLA. What, Blanche? *(Her face turns anxious.)*

BLANCHE. *(By head of bed.)* Well, Stella—you're going to reproach me. I know that you're bound to reproach me—but before you do—take into consideration—you left! *(Crosses d. l. of Stella.)* I stayed and struggled! You came to New Orleans and looked after yourself! I stayed at Belle Reve and tried to hold it together! I'm not meaning this in any reproachful way, but *all* the burden descended on *my* shoulders.

STELLA. The best I could do was make my own living, Blanche.

BLANCHE. *(Beginning to shake with a new intensity.)* I know, I know. But you are the one that abandoned Belle Reve, not I! I stayed and fought for it, bled for it, almost died for it!

STELLA. Stop this hysterical outburst and tell me what's happened? What do you mean fought and bled? What kind of—?

BLANCHE. I knew you would, Stella. I knew you would take this attitude about it!

STELLA. About—what?—Please?

BLANCHE. The loss—the loss...

STELLA. Belle Reve? Lost, is it?

BLANCHE. Yes, Stella.

> *A train passes noisily along the L&N tracks outside. [There is no long pause in dialogue for train effect.] Blanche crosses into living room to her purse on table, gets out small bottle of cologne, dabs a bit of it behind her ears.*

STELLA. *(Rising, crossing to above L. seat, looks at Blanche.)* But how did it go? What happened?

BLANCHE. You're a fine one to ask me how it went!

STELLA. *(A step nearer.)* Blanche!

BLANCHE. You're a fine one to stand there *accusing me* of it!

STELLA. *(Sitting on L. seat, facing Blanche.)* Blanche!

BLANCHE. *(Facing Stella.)* I, I, I took the blows on my face and my body! All of those deaths! The long parade to the graveyard! Father, Mother! Margaret—that dreadful way! So big with it she couldn't be put in a coffin! But had to be burned like rubbish! You just came home in time for the funerals. And funerals are pretty compared to deaths. Funerals are quiet, but deaths—not always. Sometimes their breathing is hoarse, sometimes it rattles, sometimes they cry out to you, Don't let me go! Even the old sometimes say, Don't let me go! As if you were able to stop them! Funerals are quiet with pretty flowers. And oh, what gorgeous boxes they pack them away in! Unless you were there at the bed when they cried out, Hold me! You'd never suspect there was the struggle for breath and bleeding. You didn't dream, but I saw! *Saw! Saw!* And now you sit there telling me with your eyes that I let the place go.

> *Stella crosses—Blanche follows, holds her.*

How in hell did you think all that sickness and dying was paid for?

> *Blanche stands at Stella's shoulder.*

Death is expensive, Miss Stella! And old Cousin Jessie, right after Margaret's, hers! Why, the Grim Reaper had put up his tent on our doorstep!—Stella! Belle Reve was his headquarters! Honey, that's how it slipped through my fingers! Which of them left us a fortune? Which of them left us a cent of insurance, even? Only poor Jessie— one hundred to pay for her coffin! That was all, Stella! And I with my pitiful salary at the school!

Stella breaks a step L.

Yes, accuse me! Stand there thinking I let the place go! I let the place go! Where were *you*? In bed with your Polack!

STELLA. Blanche! You be still! That's enough! *(Goes to bathroom door.)*

BLANCHE. *(Moving in close to Stella.)* Where are you going?

STELLA. *(Pausing on steps leading to bathroom.)* I'm going into the bathroom to wash my face.

BLANCHE. *(Trying to pull Stella back.)* Oh, Stella, Stella, you're crying!

STELLA. Does that surprise you?

BLANCHE. Forgive me—I didn't mean to—

> *Sound of men's voices heard from off R. Stella goes into bathroom, closing door behind her. When men appear, and Blanche realizes it must be Stanley returning, she moves uncertainly from bathroom door to dressing table, looking apprehensively toward front door. Stanley enters D. R., followed by Steve and Mitch. Stanley pauses near door, Steve by foot of spiral stair, and Mitch is slightly above and to R. of them, about to go out U. R. As men enter, we hear some of following dialogue.*

STANLEY. Is that how he got it?

STEVE. Sure that's how he got it.—He hit the old weather-bird for three hundred bucks on a six-number-ticket.

MITCH. Don't tell him those things; he'll believe it.

> *Mitch starts out U. R.*

STANLEY. *(Restraining Mitch.)* Hey, Mitch—come back here.

> *Dialogue resumes as follows. Blanche, at sound of voices, retires U. L. in bedroom. Picks up Stanley's photo from dressing table, looks at it, puts it down. When Stanley enters apartment, she darts U. L., hides behind screen at head of bed.*

STEVE. *(To Stanley and Mitch.)* Hey, are we playin' poker tomorrow?

STANLEY. Sure—at Mitch's.

> *Mitch, hearing this, returns quickly to stair rail, D. R.*

MITCH. No—not at my place. My mother's still sick!

STANLEY. Okay, at my place...

Mitch starts out again.

But you bring the beer!

> *Mitch pretends not to hear, calls out "Good night, all," and goes out U. R., singing. Eunice's voice is heard from above.*

EUNICE. Break it up down there!

> *Stanley reminds Mitch again to bring beer.*

I made the spaghetti dish, and I ate it myself!

STEVE. *(Speaking as he goes upstairs; his comments are punctuated with various colorful expletives from Eunice.)* I told you and phoned you that we was playin' Jack's Beer...

EUNICE. You never phoned me once!

STEVE. Told you at breakfast, phoned you at lunch!

EUNICE. Never mind! Why don't you get yourself home once in a while?

STEVE. God damn it! Do you want it in the newspaper?

> *Steve disappears upstairs. Door slams shut above. Stanley has entered his apartment, closing door behind him. Notices meat on table in living room, takes it to icebox. Blanche moves to door between rooms, looking at Stanley.*

BLANCHE. *(Advancing to below couch.)* You must be Stanley. I'm Blanche.

STANLEY. *(Taking off bowling jacket.)* Stella's sister?

BLANCHE. Yes.

STANLEY. *(Moving toward her; Blanche shrinks back a bit.)* H'lo. Where's the little woman?

> *He passes below Blanche and goes into bedroom, leaves coat in closet.*

BLANCHE. In the bathroom.

STANLEY. Oh. Didn't know you were coming in town. *(Crossing to kitchen cabinet.)* Where you from, Blanche?

BLANCHE. Why—I—live in Laurel.

STANLEY. *(Bringing liquor bottle and glass to table.)* In Laurel, huh? Oh, yeah. Yeah, in Laurel, that's right. Not in my territory.

He holds up bottle to observe its depletion.

Liquor goes fast in hot weather. Have a shot? *(Pours a drink.)*

BLANCHE. No—I—rarely touch it.

STANLEY. *(Smiling at Blanche.)* Some people rarely touch it, but it touches them often. *(Drinks.)*

BLANCHE. *(Faintly.)* Ha-ha.

STANLEY. *(Leaving drink and bottle on table, crosses again above Blanche.)* My shirt's stickin' to me. Do you mind if I make myself comfortable?

He stands below bed, taking off his shirt.

BLANCHE. *(Moving toward her purse on table.)* Please, please do.

STANLEY. Be comfortable. That's my motto up where I come from.

BLANCHE. It's mine, too.

She has picked up her purse and looks in it.

It's hard to stay looking fresh in hot weather. I haven't washed or even powdered—and— *(Looks at his half-naked figure.)* Here you are!

She puts cologne-soaked handkerchief to her face, turns away.

STANLEY. *(Picking up T-shirt from radio table and putting it on.)* You know you can catch cold sitting around in damp things, especially when you've been exercising hard like bowling is. You're a teacher, aren't you?

BLANCHE. *(Facing Stanley in C. of living room; neither moves.)* Yes.

STANLEY. What do you teach?

BLANCHE. English.

STANLEY. I never was a very good English student. How long are you here for, Blanche?

BLANCHE. I—don't know yet.

STANLEY. You going to shack up here?

BLANCHE. I thought I would if it's not inconvenient to you-all.

STANLEY. Good.

BLANCHE. Traveling wears me out.

STANLEY. Well, take it easy.

A cat screams off R. and Blanche jumps involuntarily toward

21

Stanley, who is amused.

BLANCHE. What's that?

STANLEY. Them's cats!

He grins. Starts into bedroom, imitating a cat.
(Going to bathroom door, calling.) Hey, Stella!

STELLA. *(From bathroom.)* Yes, Stanley!

STANLEY. Haven't fallen in, have you?

In living room Blanche moves a step D. R., uncertainly. Stanley, moving U. L. to closet, turns back to Blanche.

I'm afraid I'll strike you as being the unrefined type. Stella's spoke of you a good deal.

He goes into closet now—calling back to Blanche.

You were married once, weren't you?

BLANCHE. Yes, when I was quite young.

STANLEY. What happened?

BLANCHE. The boy—the boy died.

Distant lilt of the "Varsouviana" is heard. Blanche, listening to music, moves choppily to L. seat.

I'm afraid I'm—going to be sick.

Blanche sits on L. seat. Music grows more insistent. She tries to deny the sound, looking fearfully about her, as the lights dim. When music reaches a crescendo, she suddenly leaps to her feet, pressing her hands against her ears. The lights fade out quickly, and curtain down. Cut "Varsouviana."

In darkness, the sound of the jazz band playing a blues number comes up full. They play through change.

SCENE 2

Six o'clock the following evening. Blanche is in bathroom, taking a bath. Stella, attired in a slip, is seated at dressing table in bedroom, completing her toilette. Her dress is on back of chair by dressing table. Blanche's trunk has arrived and is placed near L. end of her daybed in living room. It is open and offers a view of some rather impressive, if gaudy, wardrobe. On chair above living room table, some of Blanche's dresses have been carelessly dropped. A heart-shaped jewel box full of jewels, a rhinestone tiara, and a perfume atomizer lie on table. Three-panel screen that had occupied upper L. corner of living room in the opening scene now stands folded against head of bed in bedroom. Stella's hat lies on the bed. Her gloves and bag are on dressing table.

AT RISE: *The street is lighted, and Stanley appears from U. L., behind gauze wall, crossing to D. R. in company of Pablo Gonzales, one of his friends. They carry lunch pails. Stanley also carries a newspaper. They are followed by Steve and a man, who pass across through street and out U. R. A woman with a basket follows men across and goes out U. R. The sound of the jazz music diminishes behind dialogue. Stanley says goodbye to Pablo D. R., and Pablo goes out D. R. Stanley comes into living room, closing door behind him. Puts newspaper and lunch box down on icebox, notices dresses on back of chair.*

STANLEY. *(To Stella.)* Hiyah, sweetheart.

STELLA. *(Jumping up.)* Oh, Stanley!

STANLEY. *(Indicating dresses, looking at trunk.)* What's all this monkey doings?

STELLA. Oh, Stan!

She runs into his arms and kisses him, which he accepts with lordly composure and pats her behind familiarly.

I'm taking Blanche to Galatoire's for supper and then to a show because it's your poker night.

On "Galatoire's" music cuts off. They are standing U. R. in living room.

STANLEY. How about my supper, huh? I'm not going to no Galatoire's for supper.

STELLA. *(Kneels on chair by Stanley.)* I put you a cold plate on ice.

STANLEY. *(Going to icebox.)* Well…

STELLA. I'm going to try to keep Blanche out till the party breaks up, because I don't know how she would take it…

Stanley has taken a plate from icebox and steps down to table, showing it to Stella. Plate contains some cold ham and a couple of slices of liverwurst.

STANLEY. Isn't that just dandy! *(Eats some meat.)*

STELLA. *(Kneels on chair above table.)* So we'll go to one of the little places in the Quarter afterwards, and you'd better give me some money.

She looks in his upper pocket for money, extracts some bills.

STANLEY. Where is she?

STELLA. She's soaking in a hot tub to quiet her nerves. She's terribly upset.

STANLEY. Over what?

STELLA. She's been through such an ordeal.

STANLEY. Yeah?

STELLA. Stan, we've—lost Belle Reve!

STANLEY. The place in the country?

STELLA. Yes.

STANLEY. How?

Separating money and putting some of it back in his pocket, Stella crosses into bedroom, puts money she has retained on dressing table. Her tone is vague.

STELLA. Oh, it had to be—sacrificed or something.

A pause, while Stanley considers. Stella starts for bedroom.

When she comes in, be sure to say something nice about her appearance.

Stanley comes into bedroom, starts D. L. toward bathroom, hears Blanche singing in bathroom—"My Bonnie Lies Over the

Ocean." *Moves back to a position above armchair in bedroom.*
And don't mention the baby. I haven't said anything yet, I'm waiting until she gets in a quieter condition.

STANLEY. *(Ominously.)* So?

STELLA. And try to understand her and be nice to her, Stan.

A look passes between Stanley and Stella. Stella puts on dress.
She wasn't expecting to find us in such a small place. You see, I'd tried to gloss things over a little in my letters.

STANLEY. *(Sitting in armchair, feet on backless chair.)* So?

Stella crosses to him, standing just at his L.

STELLA. And admire her dress, and tell her she's looking wonderful. That's important to Blanche. *(Kisses Stanley, takes a step L., fixes dress.)* Her little weakness!

STANLEY. Yeah. I get the idea. Now let's skip back a little to where you said the place was disposed of.

Blanche stops singing.

STELLA. Oh!—yes…

STANLEY. *(Grabbing a corner of Stella's dress and restraining her as she starts to move L.)* How about that? Let's have a few more details on that subjeck.

STELLA. It's best not to talk much about it until she's calmed down.

STANLEY. So that's the deal, huh? Sister Blanche cannot be annoyed with business details right now!

STELLA. *(Tying her dress belt.)* You saw how she was last night.

STANLEY. Um-huh, I saw how she was. Now let's have a gander at the bill of sale.

STELLA. I haven't seen any.

STANLEY. What do you mean to tell me!—She didn't show you no papers, no deed of sale or nothing like that?

STELLA. *(Turning away to dressing table, finishes dressing.)* It seems like it wasn't sold.

STANLEY. Well, what in hell was it, then, give-away? To charity?

STELLA. *(Taking step toward bathroom door.)* Shh! She'll hear you.

25

STANLEY. I don't care if she hears me. *(Rising.)* Let's see the papers!

STELLA. *(Directly to him.)* There weren't any papers, she didn't show any papers, I don't care about papers! *(Crosses to dresser chair.)*

STANLEY. *(Catching her arm.)* Listen; did you ever hear of the Napoleonic Code?

> *Breaking free, Stella sits at dressing table, powders nose.*

STELLA. No, Stanley, I haven't heard of the Napoleonic Code.

STANLEY. *(Moving above dressing table, leans against it, looking down at Stella.)* Let me enlighten you on a point or two.

STELLA. Yes?

STANLEY. In the State of Louisiana we have what is known as the Napoleonic Code, according to which what belongs to the wife belongs to the husband also and vice versa. For instance, if I had a piece of property, or you had a piece of property—

> *Stella persists in using powder puff, which Stanley takes from her firmly, puts it down on dressing table.*

STELLA. My head is swimming!

STANLEY. All right. I'll wait till she gets through soaking in a hot tub and then I'll inquire if *she's* acquainted with the Napoleonic Code. *(Crosses c., then into living room.)* It looks to me like you've been swindled, baby, and when you get swindled under the Napoleonic Code, I get swindled, *too*. And I don't like to be *swindled*.

STELLA. *(Rises, crossing to his L.)* There's plenty of time to ask her questions later, but if you do now she'll go to pieces again. I don't understand what happened to Belle Reve, but you don't know how ridiculous you are being when you suggest that my sister or I or anyone else of our family could have perpetrated a swindle on anyone.

STANLEY. Then where's the money, if the place was sold?

STELLA. Not sold—*lost, lost!*

> *Stella starts back to dressing table. Stanley follows quickly, grabs her, pulls her back into living room, passing her below him to a position R. of Blanche's trunk.*

(Protesting.) Stanley!

26

STANLEY. *(Pulling some [three] dresses from trunk, tossing them on couch.)* Will you just open your eyes to this stuff! You think she got them out of a teacher's pay?

STELLA. *(Gathering up clothes from couch.)* Hush!

STANLEY. *(Extracting more garments from trunk.)* Look at these feathers and furs that she comes here to preen herself in! What's this here? A solid gold dress I believe!

> *He holds up gold dress. Stella takes it from him.*

And this one.

> *He flings out another dress.*

What is these here? Fox pieces?

> *Holds up a white fox-fur piece. She reaches for it. He grabs her and talks into her face.*

Genuine fox-fur pieces a half a mile long! Where are *your* fox-pieces, Stella? Bushy snow-white ones, no less! Where are your white fox-pieces?

STELLA. *(Taking fur.)* Those are inexpensive summer furs that Blanche has had a long time.

> *Stella goes to trunk and commences stuffing dresses back into it.*

STANLEY. *(Moving D. R. in living room.)* I got an acquaintance who deals in this sort of merchandise. I'll have him in here to make an appraisal of it.

STELLA. Don't be such an idiot, Stanley.

> *She takes fur from him, returns it to trunk.*

STANLEY. *(Looking after Stella.)* I'm willing to bet you there's a thousand dollars invested in this stuff here.

> *He spies heart-shaped jewel box out of the corner of his eye.*

And what have we here? The treasure chest of a pirate?

> *He moves to table, flips open jewel box.*

STELLA. *(Hurrying to Stanley.)* Oh, Stanley!

STANLEY. *(Holding her away, fishes out jewels from box.)* Pearls! Ropes of them! What is this sister of yours, a deep-sea diver? *(Holding up bracelet, after dumping pearls on table.)* Bracelets of solid gold! Where are your pearls and gold bracelets?

Stella takes bracelet from him, crosses to above table, puts it in jewel box.

STELLA. Shh! Be still, Stanley!

STANLEY. *(Picking up tiara from table.)* And what is this—diamonds? A crown for an empress! *(Moves L. C., holding up tiara.)*

STELLA. *(Restoring jewels to box.)* A rhinestone tiara she wore to a costume ball.

STANLEY. What's rhinestone?

STELLA. *(Taking tiara from him, putting it in jewel box.)* Next door to glass.

STANLEY. Are you kidding? *(Crosses to above Stella.)* I have an acquaintance that works in a jewelry store. He's coming up here to make an appraisal of this. *(Moves to trunk, pulls out all clothes again, holding them high.)* Here's your plantation or what was left of it, here!

STELLA. *(Going to him, takes clothes, restores them to trunk.)* You have no idea how stupid and horrid you're being. Now leave that trunk alone before she comes out of the bathroom!

STANLEY. *(Moving a bit D. R.)* The Kowalskis and the DuBois have different notions.

STELLA. *(Angrily.)* Indeed they have, thank heavens!

Stella goes into bedroom, gets her hat and bag.

I'm going outside. *(Moving to Stanley.)* You come out with me while Blanche is getting dressed.

STANLEY. Since when do you give me orders?

Blanche opens bathroom door—turns back into bathroom to pick up dress.

STELLA. *(Facing him.)* Are you going to stay here and insult her?

STANLEY. You're damn tootin' I'm goin' to stay here.

He sits on table. Takes out cigarette, lights it. Takes out another, puts it behind his ear. Stella hurries out front door, leaving it open. She stands D. R. on porch and lights cigarette, which she has taken from her purse. Blanche opens bathroom door and emerges, wearing wrapper. She carries a filmy dress and purse.

Moves to door between rooms.

BLANCHE. *(Airily.)* Hello, Stanley! Here I am, all freshly bathed and scented, and feeling like a brand-new human being! *(Puts purse down on L. seat.)*

STANLEY. That's good.

BLANCHE. *(A step R.)* Excuse me while I slip on my pretty new dress!

> *She drops dress on couch, goes to curtain—places hand on draw-cord.*

STANLEY. *(Not getting hint.)* Sure, go right ahead, Blanche.

> *Realizing what she wants, he rises, crosses into bedroom. Blanche stands modestly upstage by her trunk to let Stanley pass, then closes curtains between rooms as she says, "Thank you." Sees trunk has been disturbed.*

BLANCHE. *(Taking off wrapper, putting on her dress.)* I understand there's to be a little card party to which we ladies are cordially *not* invited!

STANLEY. *(Ominously.)* That's right!

BLANCHE. Where's Stella? *(Surveys her disordered wardrobe in trunk.)*

STANLEY. Out on the porch.

> *Blanche puts on her dress. After quick look at porch:*

BLANCHE. I'm going to ask a favor of you in a moment.

> *Stella moves R. of spiral stair, facing R., and leans against stair rail. Stanley moves below bed, takes off jacket and drops it on bed.*

STANLEY. What could that be, I wonder?

BLANCHE. Some buttons in back! *(Opening drapes.)* You may enter!

> *She moves D. R. C. in living room. Stanley comes to a bit above her. He has a smoldering look on his face.*

(Facing Stanley.) How do I look?

STANLEY. You look okay.

BLANCHE. Many thanks! Now the buttons! *(Turns her back to him.)*

Coming to behind her, he makes clumsy attempt to fasten hooks.

STANLEY. I can't do nothing with them.

BLANCHE. You men with your big clumsy fingers. *(Looks at him.)* May I have a drag on your cig?

STANLEY. *(Giving her cigarette from behind his ear.)* Here—have one for yourself.

BLANCHE. Why, thanks! It looks like my trunk has exploded.

STANLEY. *(Lighting her cigarette.)* Me and Stella were helping you unpack.

BLANCHE. *(Moving to her trunk, picks up fur piece.)* Well, you certainly did a fast and thorough job of it.

STANLEY. It looks like you raided some stylish shops in Paris.

BLANCHE. *(Arranging dress in trunk.)* Yes—clothes are my passion!

STANLEY. What does it cost for a string of fur pieces like that?

BLANCHE. Why, those were a tribute from an admirer of mine. *(Puts on fur.)*

STANLEY. He must have had a lot of admiration.

BLANCHE. *(Posing in fur.)* In my youth I excited some admiration. But look at me now. *(Smiles at him radiantly.)* Would you think it possible that I was ever considered to be—attractive?

STANLEY. Your looks are okay.

BLANCHE. *(Laughs, puts fur back in trunk.)* I was fishing for a compliment, Stanley.

STANLEY. I don't go in for that stuff.

BLANCHE. What—stuff?

STANLEY. *(As Blanche straightens dresses in trunk.)* Compliments to women about their looks. I never met a woman that didn't know if she was good-looking or not without being told, and some of them give themselves credit for more than they've got. I once went out with a dame who said to me, "I am the glamorous type," *(Imitates girl, placing his hand daintily at back of his neck.)* "I am the glamorous type!" I said, "So what?"

BLANCHE. *(Going to table for jewel box.)* And what did she say then?

STANLEY. She didn't say nothing. That shut her up like a clam.

BLANCHE. *(Going to trunk with jewel box.)* Did it end the romance?

STANLEY. It ended the conversation—that was all.

Blanche laughs, puts jewel box in trunk.

Some men are took in by this Hollywood-glamour stuff and some men are not.

BLANCHE. *(At trunk; facing Stanley.)* I'm sure you belong in the second category.

STANLEY. That's right.

BLANCHE. I cannot imagine any witch of a woman casting a spell over you.

STANLEY. That's—right.

BLANCHE. You're simple, straightforward and honest, a bit on the primitive side, I should think. To interest you a woman would have to— *(Pauses with an indefinite gesture; moves downstage.)*

STANLEY. *(Following at her R.)* Lay her cards on the table.

BLANCHE. Well, I never cared for wishy-washy people. That was why, when you walked in here last night, I said to myself, "My sister has married a man!" Of course, that was all I could tell about you at the moment. *(Pats his shoulder.)*

STANLEY. *(Booming.)* All right! How about cuttin' the re-bop!

BLANCHE. *(With mock cowering, hands over her ears.)* Ouuu!

Stella, hearing commotion, rushes into room.

STELLA. Stanley! You come out here and let Blanche finish dressing!

BLANCHE. I've finished dressing, honey.

STELLA. *(Tugging at Stanley's arm.)* Well, you come out then.

STANLEY. *(Implacable, shrugs her off.)* Your sister and I are having a little talk. *(Continues looking at Blanche.)*

BLANCHE. Now, just a moment—

She moves below Stanley to L. of Stella. Stanley moves a bit L.

(Lightly, to Stella.) Honey, do me a favor. Run to the drug store and get me a lemon Coke with plenty of chipped ice in it! Will you do that for me, sweetie? Please—please—

She leads Stella to porch.

31

STELLA. *(Reluctantly.)* Yes.

> *Stella goes out D. R. Blanche closes front door and turns to Stanley. Stanley extinguishes cigarette on phone-stand.*

BLANCHE. *(As she puts out cigarette in tray on table.)* The poor little thing was out there listening to us, and I have an idea she doesn't understand you as well as *I* do... All right, now, Mr. Kowalski, let us proceed without any more digression. I'm ready to answer all questions. I've nothing to hide. What is it?

> *She sprays herself with atomizer she picks up from table.*

STANLEY. *(Moving closer to her; patiently.)* In the State of Louisiana there is such a thing as the Napoleonic Code, according to which whatever belongs to the wife belongs to the husband and vice versa.

BLANCHE. My, but you have an impressive, judicial air!

> *She sprays him with atomizer, laughs.*

STANLEY. *(Seizing her wrist.)* If I didn't know you was my wife's sister I'd get ideas about you. *(Releases her hand.)*

BLANCHE. Such as what?

STANLEY. Don't play so dumb. You know what!

BLANCHE. *(Puts atomizer on table.)* All right, cards on the table. That suits me. *(Turns to Stanley.)* I know I fib a good deal. After all, a woman's charm is fifty per cent illusion, but when a thing is important I tell the truth, and this is the truth: I haven't cheated my sister or you or anyone else as long as I have lived.

STANLEY. Where are the papers? In the trunk?

BLANCHE. Everything I own is in that trunk.

> *Stanley goes to trunk, begins rummaging in top drawer.*

What in the name of heaven are you thinking of? What's in the back of that little boy's mind of yours? Let me do that, it'll be faster and simpler!

> *She moves to trunk below him, pushing him to her R. Closes top drawer. Opens second drawer of trunk, takes out two manila envelopes, which she puts in lid. Takes tin deed-box out of second drawer.*

I keep my papers mostly in this tin box.

STANLEY. *(Looking over her shoulder into drawer.)* What's them underneath?

BLANCHE. Love letters, *("Varsouviana" is heard in background.)* yellowing with antiquity, all from one boy.

> *Stanley grabs up letters and moves R. C. Blanche, with a cry, replaces tin box in second drawer.*

Give those back to me!

> *She follows. Stanley pulls ribbon off letters, holds Blanche off as she comes at him from L. side, then from behind, in an attempt to get letters.*

STANLEY. I'll have a look at them first.

BLANCHE. *(Tugging at Stanley's arm.)* The touch of your hand insults them!

STANLEY. *(Looking at letters.)* Don't pull that stuff!

BLANCHE. *(Struggling to get letters.)* Now that you've touched them, I'll burn them!

> *Letters scatter to floor. Blanche runs above Stanley, falls to her knees, gathers letters up, ties ribbon around them.*

STANLEY. What are they?

BLANCHE. *(On her knees.)* Poems, a dead boy wrote. I hurt him the way that you would like to hurt me, but you can't! I'm not young and vulnerable anymore. But my young husband was, and I—never mind about that.

STANLEY. What do you mean by saying you'll have to burn them?

BLANCHE. *(Tying up letters.)* I'm sorry. I must have lost my head for a moment. Everyone has something he won't let others touch because of their—intimate nature...

> *She seems faint with exhaustion as she puts letters in her purse, closes it, puts it on L. arm, goes back to trunk and brings forth two large envelopes of legal papers. Stanley moves to her R. "Varsouviana" fades off. Handing Stanley one of envelopes:*

Ambler and Ambler.

STANLEY. What is Ambler and Ambler?

BLANCHE. *(Looks in tin box.)* A firm that made loans on the place. *(Piles tin box on top of envelope.)*

STANLEY. Then it *was* lost on a mortgage!

BLANCHE. That must've been what happened.

STANLEY. I don't want no ifs, ands, or buts! What's all the rest of the papers?

> *He pulls lower chair to* L. *of table, sits facing upstage, examining papers.*

BLANCHE. *(Looking into last envelope of papers at trunk.)* There are thousands of papers stretching back over hundreds of years affecting Belle Reve, as piece by piece our improvident grandfathers and father and uncles and brothers exchanged the land for their epic fornications—to put it plainly. The four-letter word deprived us of our plantation, till finally all that was left, and Stella can verify that, *(Moves to him, carrying papers.)* was the house itself and about twenty acres of ground, including a graveyard to which now all but Stella and I have retreated.

> *She pulls papers out of envelope, dumping them into his hands on table. Holds empty envelope.*

Here they all are, all papers! I hereby endow you with them! Take them, peruse them—commit them to memory, even! I think it's wonderfully fitting that Belle Reve should finally be this bunch of old papers in your big, capable hands.

> *Jazz music offstage. She drops empty envelope on table.*

I wonder if Stella's come back with my lemon Coke? *(Moves toward front door.)*

STANLEY. *(Collecting papers.)* I have a lawyer acquaintance will study these out.

> *Blanche crosses* C., *closes trunk drawer. Goes into bedroom to pick up hat and gloves from bed. Stands* D. L. *below dressing-table chair, putting on* R. *glove.*

BLANCHE. Present them to him with a box of aspirin tablets.

STANLEY. *(Still seated, somewhat sheepish.)* You see, under the Napoleonic Code—a man has to take an interest in his wife's affairs—especially now that she's going to have a baby.

BLANCHE. *(Arrested.)* Stella? Stella's going to have a baby? *(Sits in chair by dressing table. Weakly:)* I didn't know she was going to have a baby.

> *Stella appears from D. R. with Coke in a carton. Blanche hurries across to Stella, takes her out onto porch.*

(On stoop at L. of Stella.) Stella, Stella for star! How lovely to have a baby! It's all right. Everything's all right.

> *Stanley rises, takes papers into bedroom, pulls footlocker out from under bed, stuffs papers in locker, shoves it under bed, sits lumpishly on bed staring straight ahead.*

STELLA. I'm sorry he did that to you.

BLANCHE. Oh, I guess he's just not the type that goes for jasmine perfume, but maybe he's what we need to mix with our blood now that we've lost Belle Reve. We thrashed it out. I feel a bit shaky, but I think I handled it nicely, I laughed and treated it all as a joke.

> *Steve and Pablo appear from U. R., carrying case of beer.*

I called him a little boy and laughed and flirted. Yes, I was flirting with your husband! *(As men approach.)* The guests are gathering for the poker party.

> *Men pass through, tipping their hats to ladies. Pablo says "Hi, Stell." Inside, men start putting beer in icebox.*

Which way do we go now, Stella—this way? *(Points L.)*

STELLA. No, this way.

> *She leads Blanche off D. R.*

BLANCHE. *(Laughing and starting off.)* The blind are leading the blind!

VENDOR'S VOICE. Red-hot!

> *Lights fade—curtain. Jazz music swells and is heard through change.*

SCENE 3

The poker night. Music fades off quickly at rise.

Later that night. In living room, table has been pulled to L. C. Stanley, Mitch, Steve, and Pablo are gathered about table, hunched over their cards, smoking, concentrating. Table is covered with a large scrap of green baize. A low exchange of conversation passes between the men. Each has a hand of cards. In bedroom, screen has been opened so that it conceals head of bed. Stanley sits at R. end, slouching in his chair. Steve is above table, wearing his hat, sitting on inverted, empty beer case. Empty beer bottles are strung about, and a couple of liquor bottles, half-empty, are in evidence. One on table. Mitch is at L. of table, seated on L. seat, Pablo is in a chair below table, facing upstage. He is also wearing his hat. Mitch has removed his jacket, which lies on bench beside him, also his shoes.

MITCH. *(Yawning.)* What time is it?

STANLEY. What the hell difference does it make?

STEVE. He won't quit till he wins a pot. Anything wild in this deal?

PABLO. One-eyed jacks are wild.

Mitch drinks from bottle.

STEVE. *(To Pablo.)* How many cards did you take?

PABLO. Two.

MITCH. *(Rising.)* Anyone want a shot?

STANLEY. *(Taking bottle from Mitch.)* Yeah, me.

Mitch sits on L. end of table, and tucks some winnings into his pocket.

PABLO. Why don't somebody go to the Chinaman's and bring back a load of chop suey?

Cards down. Steve wins.

STANLEY. When I'm losing you want to eat. Get it off the table, Mitch. Nothing belongs on the table but cards, chips, and whiskey.

Mitch gets off table. He takes up cards.

MITCH. Kind of on your high horse, ain't you?

> *Card business. Mitch looks at his watch. Stanley deals cards. Mitch sits.*

Well, I ought to go home pretty soon.

STANLEY. Shut up.

MITCH. I got a sick mother. She don't go to sleep until I get in at night.

STANLEY. Then why don't you stay home with her?

MITCH. She says to go out, so I go, but I don't enjoy it. All the while I keep wondering how she is.

STANLEY. Aw, for the sake of Jesus, will you go home then!

MITCH. *(Tucking away his winnings, rises.)* You all are married. But I'll be alone when she goes. I'm going to the bathroom. *(Starts out L.)*

STANLEY. Hurry back and we'll fix you a sugar-tit.

MITCH. Aw—lay off!

> *Mitch returns to table, scrapes up some coins he has forgotten, then crosses through bedroom into bathroom, closing door.*

PABLO. What've you got?

STEVE. I got a spade flush. All right, boys—this game is seven card stud. Well— *(Tells joke as he shuffles cards.)* This ole farmer is out in back of his house sittin' down throwin' corn to the chickens when all at once he hears a loud cackle and this young hen comes lickety-split around the side of the house with the rooster right behind her and gaining on her fast.

STANLEY. *(Impatiently.)* Deal the cards—

STEVE. *(Resumes story and deals.)* But when the rooster catches sight of the farmer throwin' the corn he puts on the brakes and lets the hen get away and starts pecking corn. And the old farmer says, "Lord God, I hopes I never gits *that* hungry!"

> *He finishes deal. Pablo and Steve enjoy story. The three men commence playing in earnest.*
>
> *Stella and Blanche appear from D. R., come onto the porch. Blanche carries a paper lantern in a paper bag.*

STELLA. *(At closed front door.)* The game is still going on.

BLANCHE. How do I look?

STELLA. Lovely, Blanche. *(Turns to door.)*

BLANCHE. Wait before you open the door till I powder. *(Hands Stella paper bag.)* I felt so hot and frazzled. Do I look done in?

STELLA. You look as fresh as a daisy.

BLANCHE. What nonsense!

> *Blanche finishes powdering, takes back her parcel, Stella opens door. Blanche enters first, crossing to near door between rooms. Stella pauses above table.*

STELLA. Well, well, well, I see you boys are still at it! *(Crosses c.)*

STANLEY. Where you been?

STELLA. Blanche and I took in a show. Blanche, this is Mr. Gonzales and Mr. Hubbell. *(Indicates the men.)*

PABLO. Hiyah!

BLANCHE. Please don't get up.

> *Absently, Steve starts to rise, looking at his cards.*

STANLEY. *(Restraining Steve.)* Nobody's going to get up, so don't get worried.

STELLA. How much longer is this game going to continue? *(Crosses v. a bit.)*

STANLEY. *(Taking a drink.)* Till we get ready to quit.

BLANCHE. *(Moving in to L. of Steve.)* Poker is so fascinating. Could I kibitz? *(Reaches for a card.)*

STANLEY. *(Slapping at her hand.)* You could not!

BLANCHE. Excuse me!

> *She goes into bedroom. Stella has taken Pablo's coat off couch, hands it across table. Stanley whips it out of her hand, it falls to floor. Pablo yells: "My coat!," jumps up to retrieve it, placing it over back of his chair, resuming his place in game. Blanche has gone into bedroom. Puts her hat and gloves on bed and her bag and package on dressing table. Then sits on bed.*

STANLEY. Why don't you women go up to Eunice's?

STELLA. Because it's nearly two thirty. Couldn't you call it quits after one more hand?

She leans over, her back to Stanley, to unmake Blanche's bed. Stanley whacks her on the backside.

That's not fun, Stanley!

Angrily, she goes into bedroom, closing curtains behind her. Pablo laughs, and men continue playing cards.

(To Blanche, crossing to dressing table to put down purse and gloves.) It makes me so mad when he does that in front of people. *(Takes off gloves.)*

BLANCHE. I think I will bathe.

STELLA. Again?

BLANCHE. My nerves are in knots. Is the bathroom occupied?

STELLA. I don't know.

Stella goes into closet. Closet light comes on. Blanche has crossed to bathroom door, and knocks. Mitch opens door, comes out, towel in hand.

BLANCHE. Oh!—good evening!

MITCH. Hello. *(Stares at her.)*

STELLA. *(Coming out of closet to behind Blanche.)* Oh! Blanche, this is Harold Mitchell. My sister, Blanche DuBois.

BLANCHE. How do you do?

MITCH. *(With awkward courtesy.)* How do you do, Miss DuBois?

STELLA. How is your mother, Mitch?

Card game is finished.

MITCH. About the same, thanks. *(Stepping down from step to floor.)* She appreciated your sending over that custard.

He starts forward, awkwardly, but cannot pass between the girls.

Excuse me, please.

Girls ad lib—"Oh excuse me." Mitch makes his way past girls, stumbling below Stella and above Blanche to door c. The girls turn to watch him, smiling at his confusion. At door, he realizes he still is clutching towel. Overcome with embarrass-ment, he steps back into room and hands it to Stella. She puts it on lower end of dressing table. Quickly, he pushes aside curtains and returns to game. Shortly after seating himself, he gets into his shoes. Pablo deals. Girls giggle.

BLANCHE. *(Moving to c. door, unfastening dress.)* That one seems— superior to the others.

Stella puts her hat on bureau, then goes to closet, returns with bathrobe, nightgown, and slippers.

STELLA. Yes, he is.

BLANCHE. I thought he had a sort of sensitive look.

STELLA. His mother is sick.

They both giggle.

BLANCHE. *(Takes off dress.)* Is he married?

STELLA. *(Takes off shoes.)* No. *(Puts robe on chair.)*

BLANCHE. Is he a wolf?

STELLA. *(Puts on slippers.)* Why, Blanche!

Blanche giggles.

No! I don't think he would be.

BLANCHE. *(Going into closet carrying hat, gloves, and dress.)* What does—what does he do? *(While in closet, removes shoes.)*

STELLA. *(Takes off her dress at dressing table.)* He's on the precision bench in the spare parts department. At the plant that Stanley travels for.

Light out in closet.

BLANCHE. *(Coming out of closet in slip, carrying slippers.)* Is that something much?

STELLA. No. Stanley's the only one of his crowd that's likely to get anywhere. *(Puts dress in closet and returns.)*

BLANCHE. What makes you think Stanley will? *(Puts on slippers.)*

STELLA. Look at him. *(Sits on dresser chair.)*

Stanley is drinking from bottle.

BLANCHE. *(Moving to R. of Stella and standing in shaft of light from* R.) I've looked at him. *(Puts on slippers, bracing herself against armchair.)*

STELLA. Then you should know.

BLANCHE. *(Fluffing up her hair.)* I'm sorry but I haven't noticed the stamp of genius on Stanley's forehead.

STELLA. It isn't on his forehead and it isn't genius.

BLANCHE. Oh. Well, what is it, and where? I would like to know.

STELLA. It's a drive he has. Blanche, you're standing in the light.

BLANCHE. *(With a little cry, as if she didn't know!)* Oh, am I! Gracious! *(Moves U., sits on bed.)*

STELLA. *(In a suppressed aside to Blanche.)* You ought to see their wives.

BLANCHE. *(Almost laughing.)* I can imagine. Big, beefy things, I suppose.

STELLA. *(Giggling.)* You know that one upstairs...?

BLANCHE. *(Also giggling.)* Oh, that horror!

STELLA. *(Almost overcome with laughter.)* Well, one night—the plaster cracked—!

> Stella nearly collapses with laughter. Blanche is in Stella's arms, laughing her head off.

STANLEY. *(Who is losing at cards.)* You hens cut out that conversation in there!

STELLA. *(Crossing a step upstage.)* You can't hear us!

STANLEY. Well, you can hear me and I said to hush up!

STELLA. *(Looking through curtains.)* Look! This is my house and I'll talk as much as I want to!

BLANCHE. Stella, don't make a row.

STELLA. Oh, he's half drunk.

> She picks up towel Mitch left from dressing table, starts for bathroom. Blanche adjusts screen below bed.

STANLEY. *(To Mitch, who has been looking over shoulder into bedroom.)* All right, Mitch—you in?

STELLA. I'll be out in a minute.

41

She goes into bathroom, taking robe, slippers, nightgown, and towel, closing door.

MITCH. *(Pulling his attention back to game.)* What? Oh, no—I'm out!

He starts to pull himself together, lacing his shoes and getting his jacket. Blanche snaps on radio, then is adjusting screen around foot of bed in bedroom. Radio blares out a rumba.

STANLEY. *(Bellowing at bedroom.)* Who turned that on in there?

BLANCHE. *(Peeking through curtains into living room.)* I did. Do you mind?

STANLEY. Turn it off!

Blanche ignores Stanley, turns back to screen.

STEVE. Aw, let the girls have their music!

PABLO. Sure, that's good, Stanley! Leave it on!

STEVE. Sounds like Xavier Cugat!

Stanley jumps up, crosses through curtains to radio. Turns it off. Blanche cries: "Stanley!" and hides in a fold of screen. Stanley stands regarding Blanche for a long, silent pause, then returns to game. Pablo puts down his cards. Blanche goes into closet, returns wearing satin robe—combs hair, gets cigarette-holder out of purse on dressing table, moves dressing-table chair into position at lower end of dressing table, facing D. R. C. Sits. Steve, arguing with Pablo about the game:

I didn't hear you name it!

PABLO. Didn't I name it, Mitch?

MITCH. I wasn't listenin'.

PABLO. What were you doin' then?

STANLEY. He was looking through them drapes.

He is seated in his place again.

Now deal the hand over again and let's play cards or quit. Some people get ants when they win!

Mitch is on his feet, getting his jacket on.

Sit down!

MITCH. *(Leaning over table, confidentially.)* I'm going to the "head." Deal me out.

STEVE. *(Dealing.)* Sure, he's got ants now. Seven five-dollar bills in his pants pocket folded up tight as spit balls.

> *Mitch is taking Sen-Sen from small envelope in jacket pocket.*

PABLO. Tomorrow you'll see him at the cashier's window getting them changed into quarters.

> *Mitch pops Sen-Sen into his mouth, restores envelope to pocket.*

STANLEY. And when he goes home, he'll deposit them one by one in a piggy-bank.

STEVE. *(Dealing.)* All right, boys—this game is Spit in the Ocean.

> *Men resume their play. Mitch moves to pillar beside curtains, knocks timidly.*

BLANCHE. Yes?

> *Mitch enters bedroom, spies Blanche. Pulls curtain closed behind him.*

Oh, hello.

MITCH. Hello.

> *Mitch makes a little gesture toward bathroom, crosses below her to bathroom door.*

Excuse me.

BLANCHE. The Little Boys' Room is busy right now.

MITCH. *(Pausing at foot of bathroom door, embarrassed.)* We've—been drinking beer. *(Crosses back toward c.)*

BLANCHE. I hate beer.

MITCH. *(Up by armchair.)* It's—a hot weather drink.

BLANCHE. Oh, I don't think so, it always makes me warmer. *(Waving her cigarette-holder.)* Have you got any cigs?

MITCH. *(Reaching for his case.)* Sure.

BLANCHE. What kind?

MITCH. *(Crossing to her l. with open case.)* Luckies.

BLANCHE. *(Taking one, fitting it into her cigarette-holder.)* Oh, good. *(Noticing case.)* What a pretty case. Silver?

MITCH. Yes. Yes, read the inscription.

BLANCHE. *(Peering at case.)* Oh, is there an inscription? I can't make it out.

> *Mitch lights match for her, moves closer.*

Oh! *(Reads with feigned difficulty.)* "And if God choose, I shall but love thee better after death!" Why, that's from my favorite sonnet by Mrs. Browning!

> *She takes light for her cigarette from match. He takes case from her, putting out match, placing it in tray on dressing table.*

MITCH. You know it?

BLANCHE. I certainly do!

MITCH. There's a story connected with that inscription.

BLANCHE. It sounds like a romance.

MITCH. A pretty sad one. The girl's dead now.

> *Card game is finished. Pablo deals new hand.*

BLANCHE. *(In a tone of deep sympathy.)* Oh!

MITCH. She knew she was dying when she give me this. A very strange girl, very sweet—very! *(Backs up to L. of armchair.)*

BLANCHE. She must have been very fond of you. Sick people have such deep sincere attachments.

MITCH. That's right. They certainly do.

BLANCHE. Sorrow makes for sincerity, I think.

MITCH. It sure brings it out in people.

BLANCHE. The little there is belongs to people who have known some sorrow.

MITCH. I believe you are right about that.

BLANCHE. I'm positive that I am. Show me a person that hasn't known sorrow and I'll show you a superficial person. Listen to me! My tongue is a little thick! You boys are responsible for it. The show let out at eleven and we couldn't come home on account of the poker game so we had to go somewhere and drink. I'm not accustomed to having more than one drink. Two is my limit—and *three!* *(Laughs.)* Tonight I had three.

44

STANLEY. *(Bellowing.)* Mitch!

MITCH. *(Looking through curtains.)* Deal me out. I'm talking to Miss— *(Looks to Blanche to supply name.)*

BLANCHE. DuBois.

MITCH. *(Repeating name into living room.)* DuBois. *(Pulls curtains back into place, turns to Blanche.)*

BLANCHE. It's a French name. It means woods and Blanche means white so the two together mean white woods. Like an orchard in spring! You can remember it by that—if you care to.

MITCH. You're French?

BLANCHE. We are French by extraction. Our first American ancestors were French Huguenots.

MITCH. You are Stella's sister, are you not?

BLANCHE. Yes, Stella is my precious little sister. I call her little in spite of the fact that she's somewhat older than I.

MITCH. Oh!

BLANCHE. Just a little. Less than a year.

MITCH. Uh-huh.

BLANCHE. Will you do something for me?

MITCH. Sure. Yes, what?

> Blanche rises, crosses to package containing paper lantern on dressing table.

BLANCHE. *(Taking lantern out of bag.)* I bought this adorable little colored paper lantern at a Chinese shop on Bourbon. Put it over the light bulb! Will you, please? *(Hands him lantern.)*

MITCH. *(Unfolding lantern.)* Be glad to.

> Card game is finished. Stanley deals.

BLANCHE. I can't stand a naked light bulb, any more than I can a rude remark or a vulgar action. *(Puts bag on bureau, u. l.)*

MITCH. *(Fussing clumsily with lantern, as if it were an accordion.)* I guess we strike you as being a pretty rough bunch.

BLANCHE. *(Crosses back to below screen.)* I'm very adaptable—to circumstances.

45

MITCH. Well, that's a good thing to be. You are visiting Stanley and Stella?

BLANCHE. Stella hasn't been so well lately, and I came down to help her for a while. She's very run down.

MITCH. You're not—?

BLANCHE. Married? No. No, I'm an old maid school teacher.

MITCH. You may teach school but you're certainly not an old maid.

BLANCHE. Thank you, sir!

Mitch crosses to below dressing table to put lantern on bulb.

I appreciate your gallantry!

MITCH. *(Look at Blanche.)* So you are in the teaching profession?

BLANCHE. *(Moves down to opposite Mitch.)* Yes. Ah, yes…

MITCH. *(Fussing with lantern, swings bracket D.S.)* Grade school or high school or—?

STANLEY. *(Bellowing.)* Hey, Mitch!

Stanley starts U. Men restrain him.

MITCH. *(Bellowing back.)* Coming!

Blanche collapses into chair by dressing table. Stanley sits, glowering, resumes game.

BLANCHE. Gracious, what lung power! I teach high school. In Laurel.

MITCH. *(Puts lantern on bracket.)* What do you teach? What subject?

BLANCHE. You guess!

MITCH. I bet you teach art or music?

Blanche laughs delicately.

Of course I could be wrong. You might teach arithmetic.

He stands below her, his hand gradually finding a place on back of her chair.

BLANCHE. Never arithmetic, sir, never arithmetic! *(Laughs.)* I don't even know my multiplication tables! No, I have the misfortune of being an English instructor. I attempt to instill a bunch of bobby-soxers and drug-store Romeos with a reverence for Hawthorne and Whitman and Poe!

MITCH. I guess that some of them are more interested in other things. *(Hand rests on back of her chair.)*

BLANCHE. How very right you are! Their literary heritage is not what they treasure above all else! But they're sweet things! And in the spring, it's touching to notice them making their first discovery of love! As if nobody had ever known it before!

> *They laugh together. Blanche puts her hand on Mitch's. Mitch mutters, "Excuse me," and steps back, just as Stella opens bathroom door. He is in her way, and turns around rather foolishly, nearly bumping first into Stella, then almost backing into Blanche, who rises and looks at lantern.*

Oh, have you finished?

MITCH. Hm? *(Notices lantern.)* Oh, yes! *(Starts to switch on bracket.)*

BLANCHE. No. Wait! I'll turn on the radio!

> *She crosses to radio, turns it on, it plays "Wien! Wien!"*

Turn on the light above now!

> *Mitch snaps on light.*

Oh, look! We've made enchantment!

> *Blanche begins to dance about the room to music. Stella, standing in bathroom door, applauds. Mitch sings and sways to music, enjoying the impromptu completely.*

STANLEY. *(Declaring hand.)* Three bullets! You dirty greaser!

PABLO. Straight! I got you!

> *Stanley leaps up from poker game, rushes through curtains, begins pulling radio out of its socket.*

BLANCHE. Stella!

STELLA. *(Shouting at Stanley, rushes across to below him.)* Stanley! What are you doing to my radio?

> *He pulls it free, crosses to window below bathroom, and throws it out, Stella clutching at him from behind. He says, "Get the hell out of my way!," throws her off.*

Drunk—drunk—animal thing, you!

> *Blanche opens drapes between rooms. Mitch argues with Stanley about radio. Stella rushes into living room, shoving*

at Steve, then pushing Pablo. Men rise, Stella returns upstage, pushes Steve.

STEVE. Take it easy, Stella!

In bedroom, Stanley has stopped below Mitch to tell him, "That's the last time you'll play the radio during my poker game!"

STELLA. *(Pushing Steve and Pablo over R.)* All of you—please go home! If any one of you have one spark of decency in you—

Stanley hears rumpus in living room and charges in. Steve stops him. Stanley pushes Steve aside.

BLANCHE. *(By pillar.)* Stella, watch out, he's—!

Stanley takes after Stella, who retreats behind door U. R. Men quickly follow to pull him off.

STEVE. Take it easy, Stanley. Easy, fellow—

STELLA. You lay your hands on me and I'll—

Sound of a blow struck behind door. Stella cries out. Blanche screams, clutches Mitch's arm, urging him to help Stella. Mitch hurries into living room to aid in pulling Stanley off Stella.

BLANCHE. *(Shrilly, to Mitch.)* My sister is going to have a baby!

MITCH. This is terrible!

BLANCHE. *(Retreats below dressing table, stubs out cigarette in ashtray.)* Lunacy, absolute lunacy!

MITCH. Get him in here, men.

Stanley is forced back onto couch by Steve and Pablo.

STELLA. *(Staggering into doorway.)* I want to go away, I want to go away!

MITCH. *(Crossing toward Blanche.)* Poker shouldn't be played in a house with women.

BLANCHE. There are my sister's clothes! We'll go to that woman's upstairs! *(Starts for closet.)*

MITCH. *(In bedroom.)* Where is the clothes?

BLANCHE. *(Getting coat from closet.)* I've got them! Stella, Stella, precious! Dear, dear little sister, don't be afraid!

She crosses to Stella, puts coat on shoulders, ushers Stella up spiral stair, murmuring, "Did he hurt you?" etc., consolingly. Mitch follows them to door.

MITCH. *(Repeating.)* Poker should not be played in a house with women.

STANLEY. *(Struggling at couch, dully.)* What's the matter? What happened?

Men get Stanley to his feet. Steve is at his R., Pablo at his L. Mitch comes to R. of group.

MITCH. What happened? I'll tell you what happened. You just blew your top, that's what happened!

PABLO. *(Holding Stanley up.)* He's okay now.

STEVE. *(Holding Stanley up.)* Sure, my boy's okay!

MITCH. Put him on the bed and get a wet towel.

PABLO. I think coffee would do him more good now!

STEVE. Let's get him some cold water!

MITCH. Put him under the shower and give him plenty of cold water!

He gives Steve a shove toward L. Men pull the struggling Stanley L. toward bathroom, Mitch following and pushing. Mitch is heard through curses and groans of the struggle:

He shouldn't live with nice women! He don't deserve to! He don't know how to treat 'em! Put him under the shower!

Jazz band is heard. Men vanish into bathroom, pushing Stanley ahead of them. In bathroom, a terrific struggle, cries, oaths, a crash. Mitch emerges, shaking splashed water from his sleeves. Crossing through two rooms to front door; sadly, firmly:

Poker should not be played in a house with women.

He goes out, looks up spiral stair, exits U. R. Pablo and Steve hurry out before Stanley's violence. They gather up money from table.

PABLO. *(Taking up money and coat from back of chair.)* Let's get the hell out of here!

He rushes out door, exits D. R. with a groan. Steve follows Pablo out, starts up spiral stair. Eunice shouts from above:

49

"Steve!" Steve mutters, "Oh-oh!" and hurries out D. R. Lights in apartment are dimming. Stanley, after a moment, comes from bathroom. Looks about for Stella, moving uncertainly, weaving through the rooms. Pauses by phone. Takes it up. Tries to recall a number. Finally dials.

STANLEY. *(Muttering into phone.)* Eunice, is my girl up there? I want my girl! I'll keep on ringin' till I talk with my baby!

Slams phone back into place. Stanley stumbles out onto porch. Looks up spiral stair, throws back his head like a baying hound and bellows:

Stel-lahhhhh!

EUNICE. *(Above.)* You quit that howlin' down there an' go back to bed!

STANLEY. Eunice, I want my girl down here!

EUNICE. She ain't comin' down, so you quit! Or you'll git the law on you!

STANLEY. Stel-lahh!

EUNICE. You can't beat on a woman and then call her back! She won't come, and her goin' to have a baby!

STANLEY. Eunice—!

EUNICE. I hope they do haul you in and turn the fire hose on you the same as last time!

STANLEY. Eunice, I want my girl down here with me!

EUNICE. You stinker! You whelp of a Polack, you!

Eunice slams door above.

STANLEY. *(With heaven-splitting violence.)* STELL-AHHHH! STELL—

Stella comes down. Pauses near bottom step. Stanley falls to his knees, pressing his face into her belly. He weeps. Rises and takes her in his arms, turning onto porch. Her feet are off the ground. As Stella kisses him passionately:

Don't ever leave me… don't ever leave me… sweetheart… baby…

Lights in rooms are out, except for a feeble glow through shattered fan-light, a glimmer through paper lantern, and a shaft from open door of bathroom. Stanley carries Stella to their bed, pulls screen around them. Blanche runs down spiral stair, looks into apartment, hesitantly enters, recoils from what she sees, darts back to porch, closing door behind her. Looks about, distraught. Considers going back upstairs. Turns to Stella's door, finally leans against it with a troubled sigh. Mitch appears from U. R. Sees Blanche. Comes to rail to R. of spiral stair, leans toward Blanche. Fade off band.

BLANCHE. Where is my little sister? Stella—Stella!

MITCH. Miss DuBois...

BLANCHE. Oh!

MITCH. All quiet on the Potomac now?

BLANCHE. She ran downstairs and went back in there with him.

MITCH. Sure she did.

BLANCHE. I'm terrified!

MITCH. There's nothing to be scared of. They're crazy about each other.

BLANCHE. I'm not used to such—

MITCH. It's a shame this had to happen when you just got here. But don't take it serious.

BLANCHE. Violence! Is so—

MITCH. Set down on the steps and have a cigarette with me. *(Gets out case.)*

BLANCHE. I'm not properly dressed.

MITCH. That don't make no difference in the Quarter.

BLANCHE. Such a pretty silver case.

MITCH. I showed you the inscription, didn't I?

BLANCHE. Yes.

    Pause. She looks at him.

There's so much confusion in the world. Thank you for being so kind! I need kindness now.

FADE OUT AND CURTAIN

Street cries commence, and are heard through change. Street cries: 1 (Man)—Young fryers! 2 (Man)—Blackberries, 10 cents a quart. 3 (Woman)—Nice fresh roas'n ears. 4 (Man)—Watermelons! 5 (Man)—Irish potatoes! 6 (Woman)—Tender young snap beans! 7 (Man)—Fresh country eggs!

SCENE 4

Early the following morning.

Street-criers are still heard as the lights dim up. Stella is lounging in armchair in bedroom. Curtains closed between two rooms, which are still in disarray from poker game of night before. Stella's eyes and lips have that almost narcotized tranquility that is in the faces of eastern idols. Blanche comes down from spiral stair, opens door, and hurries into apartment. Street cries fade away.

BLANCHE. *(Entering.)* Stella?

STELLA. *(Stirring lazily.)* Hmmh?

> *Blanche utters a moaning cry, runs into bedroom, stands beside Stella in a rush of hysterical tenderness.*

BLANCHE. Baby, my baby sister!

STELLA. *(Drawing away.)* Blanche, what is the matter with you?

BLANCHE. *(Looking about.)* He's left?

STELLA. Stan? Yes.

BLANCHE. Will he be back?

STELLA. He's gone to get the car greased. Why?

BLANCHE. Why!—I've been half-crazy, Stella! When I found out you'd been insane enough to come back in here after what happened!—I started to rush in after you.

STELLA. I'm glad you didn't.

BLANCHE. What on earth were you thinking of?

Stella makes an indefinite gesture.

Answer me! What? What?

STELLA. Please, Blanche! Sit down and stop yelling.

BLANCHE. *(Sitting on stool in front of Stella, takes her hand.)* All right, Stella. I will repeat the question quietly now. How could you come back in this place last night? Why, you must have slept with him!

STELLA. *(Gets up in a calm, leisurely way; stretches.)* Blanche, I'd forgotten how excitable you are. You're making much too much fuss about this.

She goes to dressing-table chair.

BLANCHE. Am I?

STELLA. *(Kneeling in chair, looking in mirror.)* Yes, you are, Blanche. I know how it must have seemed to you, and I'm awful sorry it had to happen, but it wasn't anything as serious as you seem to take it.

Blanche rises and moves upstage above L. end of armchair.

In the first place when men are drinking and playing poker anything can happen. It's always a powder-keg. *(Rubs her head comfortably.)* He didn't know what he was doing… He was as good as a lamb when I came back and he's really very, very ashamed of himself.

BLANCHE. And that—that makes it all right?

STELLA. No, it isn't all right for anybody to make such a terrible row, but—people do sometimes. Stanley's always smashed things. Why, on our wedding night—soon as we came in here—he snatched off one of my slippers and rushed about the place smashing the light bulbs with it.

BLANCHE. He did—*what?*

STELLA. *(Arranging dressing-table chair to face mirror as she sits in it.)* He smashed all the light bulbs with the heel of my slipper! *(Laughs.)*

BLANCHE. *(Crossing to above dressing table.)* And you—you *let* him—you didn't *run*, you didn't *scream?*

STELLA. I was sort of—thrilled by it. *(Rises.)* Eunice and you had breakfast?

BLANCHE. Do you suppose I wanted any breakfast?

STELLA. There's some coffee left on the stove. *(Crosses u.)*

BLANCHE. You're so—matter of fact about it, Stella.

STELLA. *(Below radio table, holding up some loose wires.)* What other can I be? He's taken the radio to get it fixed. *(Gurgles pleasantly.)* It didn't land on the pavement, so only one tube was smashed.

BLANCHE. And you are standing there smiling!

STELLA. *(Puts wires back.)* What do you want me to do? *(Moves screen to head of bed—folds and stacks it there.)*

BLANCHE. *(Sits on bed.)* Pull yourself together and face the facts.

STELLA. *(Sits beside Blanche on bed.)* What are they, in your opinion?

BLANCHE. In my opinion? You're married to a madman.

STELLA. No!

BLANCHE. Yes, you are, your fix is worse than mine is! Only you're not being sensible about it. I'm going to *do* something. Get hold of myself and make a new life!

STELLA. Yes?

BLANCHE. But you've given in. And that isn't right, you're not old! You can get out.

STELLA. *(Slowly and emphatically.)* I'm not in anything I want to get out of.

BLANCHE. *(Incredulously.)* What—Stella?

> Stella rises. Crosses below to door between rooms.

STELLA. I said I am not in anything I have a desire to get out of. *(Surveys mess in living room.)* Look at the mess in this room!—And those empty bottles!

> She moves above and around table, picking up cards and putting them down. Blanche follows to c. door.

They went through two cases last night! He promised this morning he was going to quit having these poker parties, but you know how long such a promise is going to keep. *(Crossing to L. of Blanche at c.)* Oh, well, it's his pleasure, like mine is movies and bridge. People have got to tolerate each other's habits, I guess.

BLANCHE. *(Who has paused just below her trunk.)* I don't understand you.

Stella whinnies pleasantly, moves U. R. for broom.

I don't understand your indifference. Is this a Chinese philosophy you've—cultivated? *(Moves after Stella.)*

STELLA. *(Turning to Blanche, swaying broom idly in her hands, straw end in front of Blanche's face.)* Is what—what?

BLANCHE. *(Speaking with difficulty as Stella whirls broom before her eyes.)* This—shuffling about and mumbling—"One tube smashed—beer bottles—mess in the kitchen!"—as if nothing out of the ordinary had happened. Are you deliberately shaking that thing in my face?

STELLA. No.

BLANCHE. *(Pushing broom aside.)* Stop it! Put it down! I won't have you cleaning up after him!

STELLA. Then who's going to do it? Are you? *(Hands broom to Blanche.)*

BLANCHE. *(Dropping broom behind trunk.)* I—? I!

Business used by Stella in tidying up the room may vary slightly: The example herein often holds true.

STELLA. No, I didn't think so. *(Moves below table, starts gathering up cards.)*

BLANCHE. *(In corner of trunk.)* Oh, let me think, if only my mind would function!—We've got to get hold of some money, that's the way out!

STELLA. *(Gathering up cards.)* I guess that money is always nice to get hold of.

BLANCHE. *(Comes to above table.)* Now listen to me. I have an idea of some kind. Do you remember Shep Huntleigh?

STELLA. *(Puts cards in drawer of table.)* No. *(Kneels by table, gathers up bottles.)*

BLANCHE. Of course you remember Shep Huntleigh. I went out with him at college and wore his pin for a while. Well—

STELLA. Well?

BLANCHE. I ran into him last winter. You know I went to Miami during the Christmas holidays?

STELLA. No.

BLANCHE. Well, I did. I took the trip as an investment, thinking I'd meet someone with a million dollars.

Stella rises, takes bottles to kitchen cabinet.

STELLA. Did you?

BLANCHE. Yes, I ran into Shep Huntleigh—I ran into him on Biscayne Boulevard on Christmas Eve about dusk...getting into his car—

Stella places lower chair D. R.

Cadillac convertible, must have been a block long!

STELLA. *(Places upper chair in original position.)* I should think it would have been inconvenient in traffic!

BLANCHE. *(Airily, upstage.)* You've heard of oil-wells?

Stella pulls table to original position. Takes green baize off table—tucks it under arm. Replaces ashtray on table.

STELLA. Yes, remotely.

BLANCHE. He has them all over Texas. Texas is literally spouting gold in his pocket.

STELLA. *(Taking beer case that has served as poker seat to U. R.—also baize, which she leaves under stairs.)* My, my!

BLANCHE. Y'know how indifferent I am to money. I think of money only in terms of what it does for you. But he could do it, he could certainly do it!

STELLA. Do what, Blanche?

BLANCHE. *(Turning to Stella from corner of trunk.)* Why—set us up in a—shop!

STELLA. *(At cabinet.)* What kind of a shop?

BLANCHE. Oh, a—shop of some kind!—He could do it with half what his wife throws away at the races. *(A step L.)*

STELLA. Oh, he's married?

BLANCHE. *(Turning back.)* Honey, would I be here if the man

56

weren't married?

Stella laughs a bit. Blanche darts to phone.

How do I get Western Union? *(Shrilly into phone.)* Operator! Western Union!

STELLA. *(Making up Blanche's bed.)* That's a dial phone, honey.

BLANCHE. I can't dial, I'm too—

STELLA. Just dial "O."

BLANCHE. "O"?

STELLA. Yes, "O" for Operator!

Blanche considers a moment, puts phone down, goes to dressing table.

BLANCHE. Give me a pencil. Where is a slip of paper?

She gets Kleenex and eyebrow pencil from dressing table.

I've got to write it down first—the message, I mean...

She sits in armchair, using small stool as table. Stella moves into bedroom, starts making bed. Blanche, writing:

Now then—let me see—"Darling Shep. Sister and I in desperate situation."

STELLA. I beg your pardon!

BLANCHE. *(Thinking aloud.)* "Sister and I in desperate situation. Will explain details later. Would you be interested in—? Would you be—interested in..." *(Crumples Kleenex, dabs throat.)* You never get anywhere with direct appeals!

STELLA. *(Laughs.)* Darling, don't be so ridiculous! *(At chair.)*

Blanche rises, moves U. L., tosses Kleenex into wastebasket above dressing table, throws pencil onto dressing table. Picks up purse on dressing table.

BLANCHE. But I'll think of something, I've *got* to think of—*some*thing! Don't, don't laugh at me, Stella! Please, please don't laugh at me—I want you to look at the contents of my purse!

She opens purse, takes out coins.

Here's what's in it! Sixty-five measly cents in coin of the realm!

She flings coins under dressing table. Crosses to L. of armchair, purse open on L. arm.

STELLA. *(Crossing below Blanche to dressing table, takes up folded currency.)* Stanley doesn't give me a regular allowance, he likes to pay bills himself, but—This morning he gave me ten dollars to smooth things over. *(Moves to L. of Blanche.)* You take five of it, Blanche, and I'll keep the rest. *(Thrusts a bill at Blanche.)*

BLANCHE. *(Moving grandly to above armchair.)* Oh, no. No, Stella!

STELLA. *(Insisting.)* I know how it helps your morale just having a little pocket-money on you.

BLANCHE. *(Melodramatically.)* No, thank you—I'll take to the streets!

STELLA. *(Puts money in Blanche's purse.)* Talk sense! How did you happen to get so low on funds? *(Closes Blanche's purse.)*

BLANCHE. Money goes—it just goes places. *(Rubs forehead.)* Sometime today I've got to get hold of a Bromo!

STELLA. I'll fix you one now. *(Starts L. toward bathroom.)*

BLANCHE. *(Restraining her.)* Not yet—I've got to keep thinking.

STELLA. *(Back to Blanche—hands on Blanche's shoulders.)* I wish you'd just let things go, at least for a—while…

BLANCHE. Stella, I can't live with him! You can, he's your husband. But how could I stay here with him after last night, with just these curtains between us? *(Tugs at curtains between rooms.)*

STELLA. Blanche, you saw him at his worst last night.

BLANCHE. On the contrary, I saw him at his best! What such a man has to offer is animal force and he gave a wonderful exhibition of that!—But the only way to live with such a man is to—go to bed with him! And that's your job—not mine!

Turning to dressing table, Stella tidies it. Moves bracket with lantern to position close to wall.

STELLA. After you've rested a little, you'll see it's going to work out. You don't have to worry about anything while you're here. I mean—expenses…

BLANCHE. *(Behind Stella.)* Stella, I have a plan for us both to get us both out!

58

STELLA. *(Slamming a powder-box down on dressing table.)* Will you stop taking it for granted that I am in something I want to get out of?

BLANCHE. I take it for granted that you still have sufficient memory of Belle Reve to find this place and these poker players impossible to live with.

STELLA. *(Her back to Blanche, fussing at dressing table.)* Well, you're taking entirely too much for granted.

BLANCHE. I can't believe you're in earnest.

STELLA. No?

BLANCHE. I understand how it happened—a little. You saw him in uniform, an officer, not here but—

STELLA. *(Wiping picture with Kleenex.)* I'm not sure it would have made any difference where I saw him.

BLANCHE. Now don't tell me it was one of those mysterious electric things between people!—If you do, I'll laugh in your face.

STELLA. *(Violently throws paper in basket.)* I am not going to say anything more at all about it.

BLANCHE. *(Turning toward c.)* All right, then, don't!

STELLA. *(Moving to L. of Blanche.)* But there are things that happen between a man and a woman in the dark—that sort of makes everything else seem—unimportant.

     Pause.

BLANCHE. *(Crossing to back of armchair, then to Stella.)* What you are talking about is brutal desire—just—Desire!—the name of that rattle-trap streetcar that bangs through the Quarter, up one old narrow street and down another...

STELLA. *(Slightly to L. and above Blanche.)* Haven't you ever ridden on the streetcar?

BLANCHE. It brought me here—where I'm not wanted and where I'm ashamed to be.

STELLA. *(A step L.)* Then don't you think your superior attitude is a bit out of place?

BLANCHE. *(Following, restraining her.)* I am not being or feeling at all superior, Stella. Believe me, I'm not! It's just this. This is how I look at it. A man like that is someone to go out with—once—twice—three times when the devil is in you. But live with? Have a child by?

STELLA. I have told you I love him.

BLANCHE. Then I *tremble* for you!—I just—*tremble* for you…

Stella goes to armchair, sits, puts top on nail polish bottle.

STELLA. I can't help your trembling if you insist on trembling!

Pause. SOUND: *Whistle and roar of approaching train.*

BLANCHE. May I—speak—*plainly?*

STELLA. Yes, do. Go ahead. As plainly as you want to.

They are silent as train roars past. Blanche stands below bed, hands to her ears, face turned to closet, shutting out the racket. Under cover of the train's noise, Stanley enters living room from D. R. Carries a tin of oil and is covered with grease. He stands inside door, near icebox, unseen by Blanche and Stella but visible to audience, overhears the women's conversation.

BLANCHE. *(Moving D. L. a bit.)* Well—if you'll forgive me—he's *common!*

STELLA. Why, yes, I suppose he is.

BLANCHE. Suppose! You can't have forgotten that much of our bringing up, Stella, that you just *suppose* that any part of a gentleman's in his nature! *Not one particle, no!* Oh, if he was just *ordinary!*—Just—*plain*—but good and wholesome, but—*No*—. There's something downright—*bestial*—about him!—You're hating me saying this, aren't you?

STELLA. *(Coldly.)* Go on and say it all, Blanche.

BLANCHE. *(Moves in L. area.)* He acts like an animal, has an animal's habits! Eats like one, moves like one, talks like one! There's even something—sub-human—something not quite to the stage of humanity yet! Yes—something—ape-like about him, like one of those pictures I've seen in—anthropological studies! Thousands and thousands of years have passed him right by, and there he is—Stanley Kowalski—Survivor of the Stone Age! Bearing the raw meat home from the kill in the jungle! And you—*you* here— *waiting* for him! Maybe he'll strike you, or maybe grunt and kiss you! That is if kisses have been discovered yet! *(Moves upstage.)* Night falls, and the other apes gather! There in front of the cave, all grunting like him, and swilling and gnawing and hulking! His poker night!—you call it—this party of apes! Somebody growls— some creature snatches at something—the fight is on! God! Maybe we are a long way from being made in God's image, but, Stella *(Sits beside Stella, arm about her.)* —my sister—there has been *some* progress since then! Such things as art—as poetry and music—such kinds of new light have come into the world since then! In some kinds of people some tenderer feelings have had some little beginning! That we have to make *grow*! And *cling* to, and hold as our flag! In this dark march toward whatever it is we're approaching... *Don't—don't hang back with the brutes!*

> *Stanley hesitates, licking his lips. Slams shut front door and opens icebox. Blanche recoils.*

STANLEY. Hey! Hey, Stella!

> *He gets a beer from icebox, opens it. Pause and long look between the sisters.*

STELLA. *(Who has listened gravely to Blanche.)* Yes, Stanley!

BLANCHE. *(Whispering in agitation to Stella.)* Stella!

> *Blanche attempts to restrain Stella, who gets up, goes to door between rooms, opens curtains.*

STANLEY. Hiyah, Stella. Blanche back?

STELLA. *(Stepping back into bedroom, looking at Blanche.)* Yes, she's back.

> *Blanche rises, moves to door between rooms, crowding close to pillar. She is between Stella and Stanley, looking apprehensively at latter.*

STANLEY. Hiyah, Blanche.

> *He has made a step or two c. and grins at Blanche.*

STELLA. *(Looking straight at Stanley.)* Looks like you got under the car.

STANLEY. Them darn mechanics at Fritz's don't know their can from third base!

He takes drink from beer bottle. Slowly Stella moves below Blanche toward Stanley. Then, with a quick little run, she is in his arms. Stanley, as Stella throws herself fiercely at him in full view of Blanche:

Hey!

He swings her up with his body.

FADE OUT

END OF ACT I

ACT II

Scene 1

Some weeks later. The scene is a point of balance between the play's two sections, Blanche's coming and the events leading up to her violent departure. The important values are the ones that characterize Blanche: Its function is to give her dimension as a character and to suggest the intense inner life which makes her a person of greater magnitude than she appears on the surface. Music is heard as house lights dim. Fades off at rise.

AT RISE: *Blanche is seated at table in living room and has just completed writing a letter. Her purse is open on the table beside her. She bursts into a peal of laughter. Stella is seated on bed in bedroom, sewing on socks. She has sewing box and three slips. Bed is turned down.*

STELLA. What are you laughing at, honey?

BLANCHE. Myself, myself for being such a liar! I'm writing a letter to Shep. *(Picks up letter.)* "Darling Shep. I am spending the summer on the wing, making flying visits here and there. And who knows, perhaps I shall take a sudden notion to *swoop* down on *Dallas?* How would you feel about that?" *(Laughs nervously and brightly, touching her throat as if actually talking to Shep.)* "Forewarned is forearmed, as they say!"—How does that sound?

STELLA. Uh-huh…

BLANCHE. *(Continuing nervously.)* "Most of my sister's friends go north in the summer, but some have homes on the Gulf and there has been a continued round of entertainments, teas, cocktails, luncheons—"

A disturbance breaks out in apartment above.

EUNICE. *(Above.)* I know about you and that blonde!

STEVE. That's a God-damned lie!

EUNICE. You ain't pullin' the wool over my eyes! I wouldn't mind if you'd stay down at the Four Deuces it'd be all right! but you go up.

> *During fray above—on the line "I wouldn't mind," Stella says:*

STELLA. Eunice seems to be having some trouble with Steve.

EUNICE. *(Above.)* I seen you! You were chasing her around the balcony! I'm going to call the vice squad.

STEVE. *(Above.)* Don't you throw that at me, you—!

EUNICE. *(Above.)* That's for you!

STEVE. *(Above.)* Now look at what you've done.

> *Eunice, above, screams as though she had been kicked.*

BLANCHE. Did he *kill* her?

> *Door slam above. Eunice starts downstairs.*

STELLA. No. She's coming downstairs.

STEVE. You come back here.

EUNICE. I'm going to call the police. I'm going to call the police. *(Coming downstairs, rubbing her backside.)*

> *Stanley enters from D. R. He carries package of laundry, wears his good suit. Enters apartment, throws laundry on bed in living room.*

STANLEY. What's the matter with Eun-uss?

> *He has jacket off, puts it on couch, opens laundry parcel. Steve starts down from above on the run.*

STELLA. She and Steve had a row. Has she got the police?

STANLEY. Naw, she's gettin' a drink.

STELLA. That's much more practical.

STEVE. *(Bursting into living room, shirt-tail flying.)* She here?

STANLEY. *(Getting into a clean shirt, standing below couch.)* At the Four Deuces.

STEVE. That ruttin' hunk!

> *He dashes out D. R., slamming door after him.*

BLANCHE. *(Tucking Shep's letter into her purse, taking out small notebook.)* I must jot that down in my notebook. I'm compiling a notebook of quaint little words and phrases I've picked up here.

STANLEY. *(Standing above her, undoing fresh shirt.)* You won't pick up nothing here you ain't heard before.

BLANCHE. Can I count on that?

STANLEY. You can count on that up to five hundred.

BLANCHE. That's a mighty high number.

> *Stanley takes clean shirts to cabinet, opens lower drawer, tosses them in, kicks drawer shut, wads up paper laundry was wrapped in, tosses it in U. R. corner. Blanche, who has winced slightly at the noise:*

What sign were you born under?

STANLEY. *(Putting on shirt.)* What sign?

BLANCHE. Astrological sign. I bet you were born under Aries. Aries people are forceful and dynamic. They dote on noise! They love to bang things around. You must have had quite a lot of banging around in the army and now that you're out, you make up for it by treating inanimate objects with such a fury!

> *Stanley has chosen a tie from among three hanging on a hook at L. of cabinet.*

STELLA. Stanley was born just five minutes after Christmas.

BLANCHE. *(Pointing knowingly at Stanley; dabbing handkerchief with cologne.)* Capricorn—the Goat!

STANLEY. *(Buttoning shirt.)* What sign were *you* born under? *(Crosses D. back of table.)*

BLANCHE. Oh, my birthday's next month, the fifteenth of September, that's under Virgo. *(Puts cologne back into her purse.)*

STANLEY. What's Virgo?

BLANCHE. Virgo is the Virgin.

> *Stella rises.*

STANLEY. *(Contemptuously, with a look at Stella.)* Hah! *(Tucks in shirt.)*

> *Stella crosses to bureau with slips and sewing box. Puts box*

65

on bureau. Stanley moves close to Blanche, leans over her as he ties his tie.

Say, do you happen to know somebody named Shaw? Huh?

Blanche's face shows faint shock.

BLANCHE. Why, everybody knows somebody named Shaw.

Stella is at bureau.

STANLEY. Well, this somebody named Shaw is under the impression he met you in Laurel, but I figure he must have got you mixed up with some other party, because this other party *(Stella goes into closet.)* is someone he met at a hotel called the Flamingo.

BLANCHE. *(Laughing breathlessly as she touches cologne-dampened handkerchief to her temples.)* I'm afraid he does have me mixed up with this "other party."

She rises, moves below table, and leans against it, facing c. Carries purse on her L. arm.

The Hotel Flamingo is not the sort of place I would dare to be seen in!

STANLEY. *(Coming to a position directly above her.)* You know it?

BLANCHE. Yes, I've seen it and smelled it.

Stella reappears, crosses to curtains c.

STANLEY. You must've got pretty close if you could smell it.

BLANCHE. The odor of cheap perfume is penetrating.

STANLEY. *(Taking her handkerchief.)* That stuff you use is expensive?

He smells handkerchief. Tosses it back to her.

BLANCHE. *(Dropping handkerchief behind her onto table.)* Twelve dollars an ounce!—I'm nearly out. That's just a hint in case you want to remember my birthday! *(She speaks lightly, but her voice has a note of fear.)*

Stella crosses to bed, adjusts counterpane.

STANLEY. I figured he must have got you mixed up—but he goes in and out of Laurel all the time so he can check on it and clear up any mistake.

Stella crosses to dressing table. Stanley turns away upstage. Blanche closes her eyes as if to faint. Stanley picks up his jacket from couch, calls into bedroom to Stella.

I'll see you at the Four Deuces!

STELLA. *(As Stanley starts out.)* Hey! Don't I rate a kiss?

> *Steve and Eunice start in from D. R.*

STANLEY. Not in front of your sister.

> *He goes out. Stella crosses to bed for socks. Blanche, carrying her handkerchief, moves a bit upstage to below couch. On porch, Stanley meets Steve and Eunice returning. Steve's arm is around Eunice, she is sobbing luxuriously, and he is cooing love words.*

STEVE. *(Softly.)* You know I don't love those girls.

EUNICE. *(Sobbing; also sotto voce.)* I don't give a damn about those girls.

> *They start upstairs, Stanley gestures helplessly, amused, after them, then exits D. R.*

You just forget you said it.

STEVE. I love you. You know I love you. I only do that with other girls because I love you.

> *As they start up stairs, a great clap of thunder is heard. Blanche starts visibly.*

BLANCHE. *(Running to Stella, holding purse.)* Stella!

STELLA. Are you still frightened of thunder?

BLANCHE. *(Faint, her expression almost one of panic; sits on bed.)* What have you heard about me?

STELLA. Huh?

BLANCHE. What have people been telling you about me?

STELLA. Telling?

BLANCHE. You haven't heard any—unkind—gossip about me?

> *Stella takes socks to cabinet in living room—puts them in top drawer.*

STELLA. Why, no, Blanche, of course not!

BLANCHE. Honey, there was quite a lot of talk in Laurel—

STELLA. *(At cabinet.)* People talk. Who cares?

67

Thunder.

BLANCHE. *(Rises, follows Stella.)* I haven't been so good the last two years or so, after Belle Reve had started to slip through my fingers. I was never hard or self-sufficient enough. Soft people, soft people have got to shimmer and glow. They've got to put on soft colors, the colors of butterfly wings, and put a paper lantern over the light.

> *She moves to L. seat, sits. Puts down purse.*

But it isn't enough to be soft—you've got to be soft and attractive— and I'm fading now. I don't know how much longer I can turn the trick. Have you been listening to me? *(Looks back at Stella.)*

STELLA. *(Dropping her eyes to avoid Blanche's gaze, goes to icebox, gets Coke, opener, and glass.)* I never listen to you when you're being morbid.

> *She brings Coke, glass, opener to table. Thunder.*

BLANCHE. *(With abrupt change to gaiety.)* Is that Coke for me?

STELLA. *(Opening Coke.)* Not for anyone else!

BLANCHE. Why, you precious thing, you! Is it just Coke?

STELLA. You mean you want a shot in it?

BLANCHE. Well, honey, a shot never did a Coke any harm.

> *Stella starts for kitchen cabinet to get liquor, then crosses down back of table.*

Let me!

> *She crosses to Stella, leaving purse on seat.*

You mustn't wait on me!

STELLA. *(Getting bottle of whiskey and glass.)* I like to wait on you, Blanche. It makes it seem more like home.

BLANCHE. *(Touching her face with handkerchief, she goes into bedroom.)* Well, I must admit I love to be waited on.

> *Stella has poured liquor into Coke glass, looks for Blanche, starts for bedroom.*

STELLA. Blanche…honey—what is it?

BLANCHE. *(Sitting in armchair.)* You're—you're—so *good* to me! And I—

STELLA. Blanche.

BLANCHE. I know, I won't! You hate me to talk sentimental! But honey, *believe* me, I feel things more than I *tell* you! I *won't* stay long! I won't, I *promise* I—

STELLA. *(Kneeling beside Blanche at her L.)* Blanche!

BLANCHE. *(Hysterically.)* I won't, I promise, *I'll* go! Go *soon!* I will, *really!*—I *won't* hang around until he—throws me out!...

    She laughs piercingly, grabs glass, but her hand shakes so it almost slips from her grasp.

STELLA. *(Commencing to pour Coke into glass.)* Now will you stop talking foolish?

BLANCHE. Yes. Now watch how you pour— *(Takes bottle from Stella to do her own pouring.)* That fizzy stuff foams over!

    She pours. It foams over, spills. Blanche utters a piercing cry, sinks to her knees in front of chair.

STELLA. *(Shocked by Blanche's cry, takes bottle from Blanche.)* Heavens!

BLANCHE. *(Putting glass on backless chair below armchair, surveys damage.)* Right on my pretty white skirt!

STELLA. Use your hanky. Blot gently.

BLANCHE. *(Slowly recovering.)* I know.—Gently—gently.

    She blots damp spot with handkerchief.

STELLA. Did it stain?

BLANCHE. Not a bit! Ha-ha! Isn't that lucky?

STELLA. Why did you scream like that?

BLANCHE. I don't know why I screamed! *(Continuing nervously, holding Stella's hand.)* Mitch—Mitch is coming at seven. I guess I am just feeling nervous about our relations.

    Blanche speaks rapidly, breathlessly.

He hasn't gotten a thing but a good-night kiss, that's all I have given him, Stella. I want his respect. And men don't want anything they get too easily. But on the other hand, men lose interest quickly. Especially when the girl is over—thirty—They think a girl over thirty ought to—the vulgar expression is—"put out." ...And

I—I'm not "putting out." Of course, he—he doesn't know—I mean I haven't informed him—of my real age!

STELLA. Why are you sensitive about your age?

BLANCHE. Because of the hard knocks my vanity's been given. What I mean is—he thinks I'm sort of—prim and proper, you know! *(Laughs sharply.)* I want to *deceive* him just enough to make him—want me…

STELLA. *(Embracing Blanche, who crouches in her arms.)* Blanche, do you want *him*?

BLANCHE. I want to *rest!* I want to breathe quietly again! Yes—I *want* Mitch. I want him *very badly!* Just think! If it happens! I can leave here and not be anyone's problem…

> *Stanley enters from D. R. with a drink under his belt.*

STANLEY. *(Bawling out.)* Hey, Steve!

STEVE. *(Above.)* Hey!

STANLEY. Hey, Eunice!

EUNICE. *(From above.)* Hiyah, honey!

STANLEY. *(Calling into his apartment.)* Hey, Stella!

STELLA. It *will* happen!

BLANCHE. *(Doubtfully.)* It will?

STELLA. It *will!* It will, honey, *it will!* (Kisses Blanche's head.) But don't take another drink…

> *Stella starts for door. Blanche remains on floor in front of chair, staring into space. Eunice races down stairs, bellowing, "Come on, lover boy. Come on," and shouting with laughter, Steve in hot pursuit. Stanley clears for their descent. He clutches at Eunice, who eludes him with shrieks, runs out D. R. Stanley grabs Steve, holds him. Steve shrieks: "Hey! Let go!," and they struggle playfully. Stanley is thrown to steps. Steve runs out D. R. after Eunice, calling, "Hey, come back here, you little sweet patootie!" Stella comes onto porch. Stanley grabs at her.*

STANLEY. Hiyah, fatty!

> *Stella shrugs free, says, "Ah—let me go," and coolly goes*

out *D. R. Stanley, bewildered, looks after her. Then turns and looks back toward apartment, thinking of Blanche and her effect on his life. Soberly, he goes out D. R. Sound of chimes offstage. Blanche stretches and fans herself idly with a palm-leaf fan she has found lying to R. of armchair on floor.*

BLANCHE. Ah, me… ah, me… ah, me…

Young Collector enters from D. R., starts upstage, looking for likely houses, retraces his steps, looks up spiral stair, checks number on Stanley's apartment, rings bell.

Come in.

The light has grown dim. Collector enters a step. Blanche rises, comes to door between rooms, carrying her drink.

COLLECTOR. Good evening, ma'am.

Chimes fade away.

BLANCHE. Well, well! What can I do for *you*!

COLLECTOR. I'm collecting for the *Evening Star.*

BLANCHE. I didn't know that stars took up collections.

COLLECTOR. It's the paper, ma'am.

BLANCHE. I know, I was joking—feebly! *(Drops palm-leaf fan on trunk.)* Will you—have a drink?

COLLECTOR. No, ma'am. No, thank you. I can't drink on the job.

Blanche puts her drink down behind L. seat, takes up purse, looks in it.

BLANCHE. Well, now, let me see… No, I haven't got a dime! I'm not the lady of the house. I'm her sister from Mississippi. I'm one of those poor relations you've heard tell about.

She takes out cigarette and holder, puts purse on L. seat.

COLLECTOR. That's all right, ma'am. I'll drop by later. *(Starts to go.)*

BLANCHE. *(Restraining him, a step forward.)* Hey!

He turns. She puts cigarette into holder.

Could you give me a light?

71

COLLECTOR. Sure.

He takes out lighter, crosses to Blanche.

This doesn't always work.

The fact becomes apparent as he tries lighter unsuccessfully.

BLANCHE. It's temperamental?

It flares. She gets her light, touching his hand.

Ah! Thank you.

COLLECTOR. *(Moving away, pocketing lighter.)* Thank *you!*

BLANCHE. Hey!

She pauses almost at door.

What time is it?

COLLECTOR. *(Consulting wristwatch.)* Fifteen of seven, ma'am.

BLANCHE. *(Near him, facing him.)* So late? Don't you just love these long rainy afternoons in New Orleans when an hour isn't just an hour—but a little bit of eternity dropped in your hands—and who knows what to do with it? *(Crosses to him, touching his shoulders.)* You—uh—didn't get wet in the rain?

COLLECTOR. No, ma'am. I stepped inside.

BLANCHE. In a drug-store? And had a soda?

COLLECTOR. Uh-huh.

BLANCHE. Chocolate?

COLLECTOR. No, ma'am. Cherry.

BLANCHE. *(Laughs.)* Cherry!

COLLECTOR. A cherry soda.

BLANCHE. You make my mouth water.

She touches his cheek lightly and smiles. Then goes to trunk.

COLLECTOR. *(Starting out.)* Well, I'd better be going—

BLANCHE. *(Stopping him.)* Young man!

He turns. She takes a large, gossamer scarf from trunk.

Young, young, young, young—man! Has anyone ever told you that you look like a young prince out of the Arabian Nights?

COLLECTOR. No, ma'am. *(Looks away.)*

BLANCHE. Well, you do, honey lamb. Come here! Come on over here like I told you!

> *She drapes herself in scarf. He obeys like a child. Gripping his arms, looking into his face, her expression one of almost ineffable sweetness:*

I want to kiss you—just once—softly and sweetly on your mouth...

> *She does.*

Run along now! It would be nice to keep you, but I've got to be good and keep my hands off children.

> *He goes, rather dazed, to door. Faintly, waving after him, she crosses a step after him, drops scarf on couch.*

Adios!

COLLECTOR. *(On porch, looking back.)* Huh?

> *She waves again. He waves back and goes out D. R. like a child who has had a happy dream. Blanche stands in doorway. Mitch appears from U. R., carrying an absurd little bunch of flowers.*

BLANCHE. *(Gaily.)* Look who's coming! My Rosenkavalier!

> *Stiffly, he meets her on porch and offers flowers.*

No. Bow to me first!

> *Mitch is embarrassed, shakes head. She is adamant. He looks around to see if anyone is watching, then ducks a quick little bow, flowers extended to Blanche.*

And now present them!

> *He does. She curtseys low.*

Ahhhh! Merciiii!

Fade Out and Curtain

> *Jazz band plays through change.*

Scene 2

Later. About 2 A.M. Music fades away at rise. Blanche and Mitch enter from U. L., moving slowly through street. They pass the Negro woman, who is crossing from R. to L., singing a melancholy tune. Blanche carries hat, purse, and flowers. Mitch holds a ridiculous doll he has won somewhere. The utter exhaustion which only a neurasthenic personality can know is evident in Blanche's voice and manner. Mitch is stolid but depressed. They come around on porch, Blanche to a position below closed door.

BLANCHE. Well…

MITCH. *(Above pillar at R.)* Well…

Negro woman drifts out of sight and hearing.

I guess it must be pretty late—and you're tired.

BLANCHE. How will you get home?

MITCH. I'll walk over to Bourbon and catch an owl-car.

BLANCHE. *(Laughing grimly.)* Is that streetcar named Desire still grinding along the tracks at this hour?

MITCH. *(Heavily.)* I'm afraid you haven't had much fun out of this evening, Blanche.

BLANCHE. I spoiled it for *you.*

MITCH. No, you didn't, but I felt all the time that I wasn't giving you much—entertainment.

BLANCHE. I simply couldn't rise to the occasion. That was all. *(Turns D. L. on porch.)* I don't think I've ever tried so hard to be gay and made such a dismal mess of it.

MITCH. Why did you try if you didn't feel like it, Blanche?

BLANCHE. *(Looks in purse.)* I was just obeying the law of nature.

MITCH. Which law is that?

BLANCHE. The one that says the lady must entertain the gentleman—or no dice! See if you can locate my door-key in this purse. *(Hands him her purse.)* When I'm so tired my fingers are all thumbs.

MITCH. *(Rooting in purse, comes up with a key.)* This it?

BLANCHE. No, honey—that's the key to my trunk which I must soon be packing.

MITCH. You mean you are leaving pretty soon now?

BLANCHE. *(Looks at stars.)* I've outstayed my welcome.

MITCH. *(Who has found another key.)* This it?

BLANCHE. Eureka! Honey, you open the door while I take a last look at the sky.

> *Blanche stares up at the stars. Moves a bit R. Mitch unlocks door, puts key back into Blanche's purse, stands awkwardly, a bit behind her.*

I'm looking for the Pleiades, the Seven Sisters, but these girls are not out tonight. *(Spies them.)* Oh, yes, they are, there they are! God bless them! All in a bunch going home from their little bridge party... *(Turns to Mitch.)* Y'get the door open? Good boy.

> *She moves up to his L. just below door, takes purse.*

Well, I guess you—want to go now...

MITCH. *(At her R.)* Can I—uh—kiss you—good night?

BLANCHE. *(Crossly.)* Why do you always ask me if you may?

MITCH. I don't know whether you want me to or not.

BLANCHE. Why should you be so doubtful?

MITCH. That night when we parked by the lake and I kissed you, you—

BLANCHE. Honey, it wasn't the kiss I objected to. I liked the kiss very much. It was the other little—familiarity—that I—felt obliged to—discourage. I didn't resent it! Not a bit in the world! In fact I was somewhat flattered that you—desired me! But, honey, you know as well as I do that a single girl, a girl alone in the world, has got to keep a firm hold on her emotions, or she'll be lost!

MITCH. *(Solemnly.)* Lost?

BLANCHE. *(Turning away a step.)* I guess you are used to girls that like to be lost. The kind that get lost immediately on the first date.

MITCH. *(A step after her.)* I like you to be exactly the way that you

75

are, because in all my—experience—I have never known anyone like you.

Blanche looks at him gravely, then bursts into laughter, buries her head against his upstage shoulder.

—Are you laughing at me?

BLANCHE. *(Patting his cheek.)* No, no, no, honey. No—I'm not laughing at you—

She goes into apartment, he follows.

The lord and lady of the house have not yet returned, so come in.

She drops hat, purse, gloves, and flowers on table.

We'll have a night-cap. Let's leave the lights off, shall we?

Mitch closes front door. Blanche is above table, facing U.S.

The other room's more comfortable…go on in.

He moves L. toward bedroom.

This crashing around in the dark is my search for some liquor.

MITCH. *(Near C.)* You want a drink?

BLANCHE. *(Taking glasses to him and shoving him even further into bedroom.)* I want *you* to have a drink! You have been so anxious and solemn all evening, and so have I, we have both been anxious and solemn and now for these few last remaining moments of our lives together—

She has returned to cabinet and is lighting a match.

I want to create—*joie de vivre!* (Applies match to candle stuck in bottle, which she gets from cabinet.) I'm lighting a candle.

MITCH. That's good.

BLANCHE. *(Bringing lighted candle to table in living room.)* We are going to be very bohemian. We are going to pretend that this is a little artists' café on the Left Bank in Paris!

She moves toward him with bottle of liquor, which she picks up from top of cabinet.

Je suis la Dame aux Camelias! Vous etes—Armand! Do you understand French?

MITCH. *(Standing U. C. in bedroom, shrugging, laughing.)* Naw. Naw, I don't understand French.

BLANCHE. *(Coming toward him.)* Voulez-vous couchez avec moi ce soir? Vous ne comprenez pas? Ah! Quel dommage! I mean, it's a damned good thing I've found some liquor, just enough for two shots without any dividends...

She pours drinks into glasses that he holds. Mitch drinks.

MITCH. That's—good!

Blanche drinks, takes her glass and bottle to dressing table, turns to Mitch, takes his glass and doll to dressing table. Wipes hands on Kleenex she picks up from dressing table then throws into wastebasket.

BLANCHE. Sit down! Why don't you take off your coat and loosen your collar?

MITCH. I'd better leave it on.

BLANCHE. No. I want you to be comfortable.

MITCH. *(Sits in armchair.)* No—I am ashamed of the way I perspire. My shirt is sticking to me.

BLANCHE. Perspiration is healthy. If people didn't perspire they would die in five minutes.

She helps him off with his jacket.

This is a nice coat. *(Waves it gently.)* What kind of material is it?

MITCH. They call that stuff alpaca.

BLANCHE. Oh. Alpaca.

MITCH. It's very light-weight alpaca.

BLANCHE. Light-weight alpaca.

MITCH. I don't like to wear a wash coat even in summer because I sweat right through it.

BLANCHE. Oh.

She hangs coat over back of dressing-table chair.

MITCH. And it don't look neat on me. A man with a heavy build has got to be careful of what he puts on him so he don't look too clumsy.

BLANCHE. You're not too heavy.

> *She pulls backless chair to his L. and below him, sits facing him.*

MITCH. You don't think I am?

BLANCHE. You are not the delicate type. You have a massive bone-structure and a very imposing physique.

MITCH. I thank you. Last Christmas I was given a membership in the New Orleans Athletic Club.

BLANCHE. Oh, good.

MITCH. It was the finest present I ever was given. I work out there with the weights. And I swim and I keep myself fit. When I started there I was soft in the belly, but now my belly is hard. It is so hard that a man can punch me in the belly and it don't hurt me.

> *He rises.*

Punch me! Go on! *(Hits himself in belly.)* See?

BLANCHE. *(Punching him gently in belly, then laying her hand against him.)* Gracious!

MITCH. *(Moving above armchair, flexing his muscles.)* Blanche— Blanche—guess how much I weigh?

BLANCHE. Oh, I'd say in the vicinity of—one hundred and eighty pounds?

MITCH. *(Moving for her inspection.)* Oh, no. No. Guess again.

BLANCHE. Not that much?

MITCH. No: more.

BLANCHE. Well, you're a tall man and you can carry a good deal of weight without looking awkward.

MITCH. I weigh two hundred and seven pounds and I'm six feet one and one-half inches tall in my bare feet—without shoes on. And that is what I weigh stripped.

BLANCHE. Oh, my goodness, me! That's awe-inspiring!

MITCH. *(Embarrassed.)* My weight is not a very interesting subject to talk about.

> *Pause.*

What's yours?

BLANCHE. My weight?

MITCH. Yes.

> *Blanche rises, moves a bit upstage.*

BLANCHE. Guess!

MITCH. Let me lift you!

BLANCHE. *(Extending her arms daintily.)* Samson! *(Dismissing idea—then reconsiders.)* Go ahead—lift me!

> *Mitch lifts her, whirls her around downstage.*

MITCH. *(Holding her up.)* You are light as a feather.

> *He lowers her, but keeps hands on her waist. She affects demureness.*

BLANCHE. You may release me now.

MITCH. Huh?

BLANCHE. *(Gaily.)* I said, unhand me, sir.

> *Mitch tries to kiss her, fumblingly embracing her.*

Now, Mitch. Just because Stanley and Stella aren't at home is no reason why you shouldn't behave like a gentleman.

MITCH. *(Holding her close.)* Just give me a slap whenever I step out of bounds.

BLANCHE. *(Trying to get free.)* That won't be necessary. You're a natural gentleman, one of the very few that are left in the world. I don't want you to think that I am severe and old-maid school-teacherish or anything like that. It's just—well—I guess it is just that I have—old-fashioned ideals!

> *Piano is heard. Mitch releases her, crosses quickly to front door, stands with one foot on porch looking out. Blanche crosses to below trunk, adjusting dress.*

MITCH. *(His voice breaking.)* Where's Stanley and Stella tonight?

BLANCHE. They have gone out. With Mr. and Mrs. Hubbell upstairs.

MITCH. Where did they go?

BLANCHE. I think they were planning to go to a midnight prevue at Loew's State.

MITCH. We should all go out together some night.

BLANCHE. No. No, that wouldn't be a good idea.

MITCH. Why not?

BLANCHE. You are an old friend of Stanley's?

MITCH. *(With a trace of bitterness.)* We was together in the Two-forty-first.

BLANCHE. I guess he talks to you frankly?

MITCH. Sure.

BLANCHE. *(A step toward him.)* Has he talked to you about me?

MITCH. *(Closing door, turning to Blanche.)* Not very much.

> *Fade out piano.*

BLANCHE. The way you say that, I suspect that he has.

MITCH. No, he hasn't said much. *(Crosses to her.)*

BLANCHE. But what he *has* said? What would you say his attitude toward me was?

MITCH. What makes you ask that?

BLANCHE. Well—

MITCH. Don't you get along with him?

BLANCHE. What do you think?

MITCH. *(Crossing D. L. C., faces L.)* I think he don't understand you.

BLANCHE. *(Coming to L. of table.)* That is putting it mildly. If it weren't for Stella about to have a baby, I wouldn't be able to endure things here.

MITCH. He isn't—nice to you?

BLANCHE. He's insufferably rude. Goes out of his way to offend me.

MITCH. In what way, Blanche?

BLANCHE. Why, in every conceivable way.

MITCH. I'm surprised to hear that. *(Turns away from her.)*

BLANCHE. Are you?

MITCH. *(Facing her.)* Well, I—don't see how anybody could be rude to you.

BLANCHE. It's really a pretty frightful situation. You see, there's no privacy here. There's just these portieres between the two rooms. He stalks through the rooms in his underwear at night. And I have to ask him to close the bathroom door. That sort of commonness isn't necessary. You probably wonder why I don't move out? Well, I'll tell you frankly. A school teacher's salary is barely sufficient for her living expenses. I didn't save a penny last year, and so I had to come here for the summer. That's why I have to put up with my sister's husband. And he has to put up with me, apparently so much against his wishes... Surely he must have told you how much he hates me!

MITCH. I don't think he hates you.

BLANCHE. He hates me, or why does he insult me? The first time I laid eyes on him, I thought to myself, that man is my executioner! That man will destroy me!—unless—

MITCH. Blanche... Blanche—

BLANCHE. Yes, honey?

MITCH. Can I ask you a question?

BLANCHE. Yes. What?

MITCH. How old are you?

> Blanche makes nervous gesture, crosses below him to below L. seat.

BLANCHE. Why do you want to know?

MITCH. I talked to my mother about you, and she said, How old is Blanche?

> Pause. Blanche sits in L. seat. Looks at him.

BLANCHE. You talked to your mother about me?

MITCH. Yes.

BLANCHE. Why?

MITCH. Because I told her how nice you were, and I liked you.

BLANCHE. Were you sincere about that?

MITCH. *(Sits beside her.)* You know I was.

BLANCHE. Why did your mother want to know my age?

MITCH. Mother is sick.

BLANCHE. I'm sorry to hear it. Badly?

MITCH. She won't live long. Maybe just a few months, and she worries because I'm not settled. She wants me to be settled down before she—

His voice is hoarse with emotion. He looks away from Blanche.

BLANCHE. You love her very much, don't you?

Mitch nods, miserably.

I think you have a great capacity for devotion. You'll be lonely when she passes on.

Mitch looks at her, nods.

I understand what that is.

MITCH. To be lonely?

BLANCHE. I loved someone, too, and the person I loved I lost.

MITCH. Dead? A man?

BLANCHE. He was a boy, just a boy, when I was a very young girl. When I was sixteen, I made the discovery—love. All at once and much, much too completely. It was like you suddenly turned a blinding light on something that had always been half in shadow, that's how it struck the world for me. But I was unlucky. Deluded. There was something different about the boy, a nervousness, a softness, tenderness which wasn't like a man's although he wasn't the least bit effeminate-looking—still—that thing was there... He came to me for help. I didn't know that. I didn't find out anything till after our marriage when we'd run away and come back and all I knew was I'd failed him in some mysterious way and wasn't able to give him the help he needed but couldn't speak of! He was in the quicksands clutching at me—but I wasn't holding him out, I was slipping in with him! I didn't know that. I didn't know anything except I loved him unendurably but without being able to help him or help myself. Then I found out. In the worst of all possible ways. By suddenly coming into a room that I thought was empty—which wasn't empty, but had two people in it... the boy I married and an older man who had been his friend for years.

She breaks away, rises, goes upstage.

Afterwards we pretended that nothing had been discovered. Yes, we all drove out to Moon Lake Casino, very drunk and laughing all the way. We danced the Varsouviana!

"Varsouviana" is heard, fades.

Suddenly, in the middle of the dance, the boy I had married broke away from me and ran out of the Casino. A few moments later—a shot! I ran out, all did!—all ran and gathered around this terrible thing at the edge of the lake! I couldn't get near for the crowding. Then somebody caught my arm.—"Don't go any closer! Come back! You don't want to see!" See? See what? Then I heard voices say, "Allan! Allan! The Gray boy!" He'd stuck a revolver into his mouth and fired!—so that the back of his head had been—blown away!

She sways, covers her face. "Varsouviana" is heard again.

It was because, on the dance floor—unable to stop myself—I'd suddenly said—"I know! I saw! You disgust me!" And then the searchlight which had been turned on the world was turned off again and never for one moment since has there been any light stronger than this kitchen candle...

Mitch rises, goes to her, stands behind her.

MITCH. You need somebody. And I need somebody, too. Could it be you and me, Blanche?

She turns to him. Looks at him. They embrace, kiss. Cut "Varsouviana" sharply.

BLANCHE. Sometimes—there's God—so quickly!

FADE OUT AND HOUSE CURTAIN

END OF ACT II

ACT III

Scene 1

Some weeks later. The rooms have been made pathetically dainty with some of Blanche's bits of finery, pillows, fan, slipcovers, etc.

First lights to come up are those in street area. Stanley starts across to the porch area. As he crosses, lights come up in apartment. Stella is hovering over table in living room, which is set for four, decorated with party favors, colored napkins. Her approaching maternity is more evident than earlier in the play. At rise she brings birthday cake from cabinet, puts it at c. of table, then goes to cabinet, gets knives, forks, and spoons, starts placing them around table, beginning with upstage place and working to R. side, below, then to L. place, during opening dialogue of scene. Blanche is in bathroom, where she is singing scraps of a sad blues song. Blanche's trunk is closed and covered with a net drapery. Stanley enters apartment, puts lunch pail on top of icebox, surveys party set-up.

STANLEY. What's all this stuff for?

STELLA. *(Gets silver.)* Honey, it's Blanche's birthday.

STANLEY. She here?

STELLA. *(Laying silver.)* In the bathroom.

STANLEY. *(Mimicking.)* "Washing out some things"?

    Blanche sings in bathroom.

STELLA. I reckon so.

STANLEY. How long she been in there?

STELLA. All afternoon.

STANLEY. *(Mimicking.)* "Soaking in a hot tub"?

STELLA. (Unperturbed.) Yes.

Blanche stops singing.

STANLEY. Temperature 100 on the nose, and she soaks in a hot tub!

STELLA. She says it cools her off for the evening.

STANLEY. And you run out an' get her Cokes, I suppose? And serve 'em to Her Majesty in the tub?

Stella shrugs, occupied with table.

Set down here. (Indicates chair L. of table.)

STELLA. Stanley, I've got things to do.

STANLEY. Set down!

Stella crosses to behind L. chair.

I've got th' dope on your big sister, Stella.

STELLA. Stanley, stop picking on Blanche.

STANLEY. That girl calls *me* common!

STELLA. (Moving to L. of Stanley above table.) Lately you been doing all you can think of to rub her the wrong way, Stanley. Blanche is sensitive. You've got to realize that Blanche and I grew up under very different circumstances than you did.

STANLEY. So I been told. And told and told and told! You know she's been feeding us a pack of lies here?

STELLA. No, I don't—and I don't want to hear—

STANLEY. (Overlapping Stella's speech.) Well, she has, however. But now the cat's out of the bag! I found out some things!

STELLA. What—things?

STANLEY. Things I already suspected.

Blanche sings in bathroom.

But now I got proof from the most reliable sources—which I have checked on!

Bathroom door opens, Blanche pops out in her bathrobe. Goes to dressing table, picks up a drink with ice cubes, waves to Stanley in other room.

BLANCHE. Hello, Stanley!

Gaily, she hums, clinks ice in her glass, goes into bathroom, shuts door. Stella backs upstage—looks at Blanche.

STANLEY. *(Sitting above table.)* —Some canary bird, huh?

STELLA. *(Coming back to table, sits L. chair.)* Now please tell me quietly what you think you've found out about my sister.

STANLEY. Lie number one: All this squeamishness she puts on!—you should just know the line she's been feeding to Mitch. He thought she had never been more than kissed by a fellow! You know Sister Blanche is no lily!

STELLA. What have you heard, and who from?

STANLEY. Our supply-man down at the plant has been going through Laurel for years and he knows all about her, and everybody else in the town of Laurel knows all about her, she is as famous in Laurel as if she was the President—of the United States—

Blanche sings blues song in bathroom.

—only she is not respected by any party! This supply-man stops at a hotel called the Flamingo.

STELLA. What about the—Flamingo?

STANLEY. She stayed there, too.

STELLA. My sister stayed at Belle Reve.

STANLEY. This is after the home place had slipped through her lily-white fingers! She moved to the Flamingo! A second-class hotel which has the advantage of not interfering with the private social life of the personalities there! The Flamingo's used to all kinds of goings-on. But even the management of the Flamingo was impressed by Dame Blanche! In fact they was so impressed that they requested her to turn in her room-key—for *permanently!* This happened a couple of weeks before she showed here.

Blanche sings in bathroom. Stella rises, moves a step L., looks toward bathroom listening to Blanche's song. Moves D. L. in living room, head bowed. Stanley rises, moves through C. to R. of Stella.

Sure, I can see how you would be upset by this. She pulled the wool over your eyes as much as Mitch's.

He tries to put an arm around her, she shrugs him off.

STELLA. *(Turning to him.)* It's pure invention! There's not a word of truth in it!

> *Blanche sings in bathroom. Stanley takes her by the arms, faces her. Blanche is singing.*

STANLEY. Honey, I told you I checked on every single story. The trouble with Dame Blanche was that she couldn't put on her act any more in Laurel!

> *Blanche stops singing.*

They got wised up after two or three dates with her and they quit, and she goes on to another, the same old line, same old act, same old hooey! But the town was too small for this to go on forever! And as time went by she became the town character. Regarded as not just different but downright loco—nuts.

> *Blanche sings. Stella moves to D. R. chair below table. Stanley moves U. to a position behind Stella.*

And for the last year or two she has been washed up like poison. That's why she's here this summer, visiting royalty, putting on all this act—she was practically told by the Mayor to get out of town! Yes, did you know there was an army-camp near Laurel and your sister's was one of the places called "Out-of-Bounds"?

> *Moving a bit upstage C.—looking toward bathroom, Stanley then speaks to Stella directly.*

Well, so much for her being such a refined and particular type of girl. Which brings us to Lie number two.

STELLA. *(A step toward him; will hear no more.)* I don't want to hear any more!

STANLEY. She didn't resign temporarily because of her nerves! No, siree, bob! She didn't. She was kicked out before the Spring term ended—and I hate to tell you the reason that step was taken—A seventeen-year-old boy—she's gotten mixed up with! And when…

> *Blanche heard still singing in bathroom.*

STELLA. *(Head bowed over table.)* This is making me—sick!

STANLEY. *(Moving to cabinet and back to above table.)* …the boy's dad learned about it and got in touch with the high school superintendent. Oh, I'd like to have been in that office when Dame

Blanche was called on the carpet! I'd like to have seen her trying to squirm out of that one! But they had her hooked good and proper that time and she knew that the jig was all up! They told her she better move on to some fresh territory, it was practickly a town ordinance passed against her!

> *Blanche stops. Bathroom door opens, Blanche thrusts her head out, holding a bath towel about her hair.*

BLANCHE. *(In doorway.)* Stella!

STELLA. *(Faintly.)* Yes, Blanche? *(Starts for bedroom.)*

BLANCHE. Get me another bath towel to dry my hair with. I've just washed it!

STELLA. Yes, Blanche.

> *Stella gets towel from middle drawer of bureau, takes it in a dazed way to Blanche.*

BLANCHE. *(On bathroom steps, looks sharply at Stella.)* What's the matter, honey?

STELLA. *(Turning away.)* Matter? Why?

BLANCHE. You have such a strange expression on your face.

> *Stanley crosses to below trunk.*

STELLA. Oh! *(Tries to laugh.)* I guess I'm a little tired.

BLANCHE. Why don't you take a hot bath as soon as I get out?

> *Stella goes to below head of bed—hand to her back.*

STANLEY. *(From a vantage point below Blanche's trunk where he has been watching.)* How soon is that going to be, Blanche?

BLANCHE. *(Waving clean towel at him, blithely.)* Not so terribly long! Possess your soul in patience!

> *She starts into bathroom—stops as he speaks.*

STANLEY. It's not my soul, it's my kidneys I'm worried about!

> *Blanche slams door shut. Stella comes back into living room. Crosses below Stanley to above and L. of table. He leans against trunk.*

Well, what do you think of it?

STELLA. *(Turns to Stanley.)* I don't believe all of those stories, and

I think your supply-man was mean and rotten to tell them. Oh, it's possible that some of the things he said are partly true. My sister was always—flighty!

STANLEY. Yeah—flighty!

STELLA. But when she was young, very young— *(Dabs at plates and decorations, not seeing them.)* She married a boy who wrote poetry... He was extremely good-looking. I think Blanche didn't just love him but worshipped the ground he walked on! Adored him and thought him almost too fine to be human!

> *Goes to cabinet, gets small box of pink birthday cake candles.*

But then she found out—

STANLEY. What?

STELLA. *(Bringing candles to table.)* This beautiful and talented young man was a degenerate. Didn't your supply-man give you *that* information? *(Opens box of candles.)*

STANLEY. All we discussed was recent history. That must have been a pretty long time ago.

STELLA. *(Sits at table.)* Yes, it was—a pretty long time ago...

> *She starts sticking candles on birthday cake. Pause.*

STANLEY. *(Crossing D. as he looks at cake.)* How many candles you stickin' in that cake?

STELLA. I'll stop at twenty-five.

STANLEY. Is company expected?

STELLA. We asked Mitch to come over for cake and ice-cream.

STANLEY. *(Uncomfortably, after a pause.)* Don't expect Mitch over tonight.

> *Stella pauses in her occupation with candles. Looks slowly around at Stanley.*

STELLA. Why? *(Rising.)*

STANLEY. *(Turning quickly to Stella.)* Stella, Mitch is a buddy of mine. We were in the same outfit together—Two-forty-first Engineers. We work in the same plant and now on the same bowling team—

STELLA. *(Cutting in, crossing to below Stanley.)* Stanley Kowalski, did you—? Did you repeat what that—?

STANLEY. (*Cutting in.*) You're damned right I told him! I'd have that on my conscience the rest of my life if I knew all that stuff and let my best friend get caught!

He goes out onto porch.

STELLA. (*Following.*) Is Mitch through with her?

STANLEY. Well—wouldn't you be if—?

STELLA. I said, *Is Mitch through with her?*

Blanche sings in bathroom.

STANLEY. (*Facing Stella.*) No, not exactly through with her—just wised up!

STELLA. (*Taking hold of Stanley.*) Stanley, she thought Mitch was going to—going to marry her. I was hoping so, too.

STANLEY. (*Pulling her roughly around to his R.*) Well he's not going to marry her now. (*Continuing—crossing quickly to bathroom.*) Maybe he *was*, but he's not going to jump in a tank with a school of sharks! (*Calling at bathroom door.*) Blanche! Oh, Blanche! Can I please get in my bathroom?

BLANCHE. (*Answering Stanley through bathroom door.*) Yes, indeed, sir, can you wait one second while I dry?

STELLA. (*Following, distressed.*) Stanley!

STANLEY. Having waited one hour I guess one second ought to pass in a hurry.

STELLA. She hasn't got her job. What will she do?

STANLEY. (*Turning to Stella.*) She's not stayin' here after Tuesday. You know that, don't you? Just to make sure, I bought her ticket myself. A bus ticket!

He fumbles in his breast pocket to show Stella ticket.

STELLA. In the first place, Blanche wouldn't go on a bus.

STANLEY. She'll go on a bus and like it.

STELLA. No, she won't, no, she won't, Stanley!

STANLEY. *She'll go!* Period. P.S.—She'll go *Tuesday!*

STELLA. (*Slowly.*) What'll—she—do? What on earth will she—*do?*

STANLEY. Her future is mapped out for her.

STELLA. What do you mean?

She grabs Stanley's arms. Blanche sings in bathroom. Stanley frees himself from her grip.

STANLEY. *(Going to bathroom door, pounding on it.)* Hey, canary bird! Toots! Get *OUT* of the *BATHROOM!*

Stella moves close to R. of Stanley. Door opens. Blanche emerges with a gay peal of laughter, stepping into bedroom. Steam rises from bathroom.

BLANCHE. *(Carries hairbrush.)* Oh, I feel so good after my long, hot bath, I feel so good and cool and—rested!

She crosses to L. C. Stanley goes into bathroom, slamming door shut, which arrests Blanche's crossing.

STELLA. *(Sadly and doubtfully, crossing into living room.)* Do you, Blanche?

She picks up extra candles by cake and stuffs them into little candle box.

BLANCHE. *(Brushing hair vigorously.)* Yes, I do, so refreshed! A hot bath and a long, cold drink always gives me a brand new outlook on life! *(Looks at bathroom door, then at Stella.)* Something has happened. What is it?

STELLA. *(Turning away quickly.)* Why, nothing has happened, Blanche.

BLANCHE. *(Pausing, facing Stella.)* You're lying! Something has!

FADE OUT AND CURTAIN

Orchestra is heard playing through change.

*Three-quarters of an hour later. Stanley, Stella, and Blanche
are completing a dismal birthday dinner. They are seated
about table, Stanley at R., Blanche upstage, Stella at L. Stanley
is sullen. He is gnawing at a chop and licks his fingers. Stella
is embarrassed and sad. Blanche has a tight, artificial smile
on her drawn face. There is a fourth chair at table, on D.S.
side, which is vacant. Music continues behind dialogue.*

BLANCHE. *(Who is nursing a drink, speaks suddenly.)* Stanley, tell us
a joke, tell us a funny story to make us all laugh. I don't know what's the
matter, we're all so solemn. Is it because I've been stood up by my beau?

> *Stella laughs feebly.*

It's the first time in my entire experience with men, and I've had a
good deal of all sorts, that I've actually been stood up by anybody! I
don't know how to take it… Tell us a funny little story, Stanley! Something to help us out.

STANLEY. *(Licking his fingers.)* I didn't think you liked my stories,
Blanche.

BLANCHE. I like them when they're amusing, but not indecent.

STANLEY. I don't know any refined enough for your taste.

BLANCHE. Well—then let me tell one.

STELLA. Yes, you tell one, Blanche. You used to know lots of good
stories.

BLANCHE. Let me see now…

> *Fade off music.*

I must run through my repertoire! Oh, yes, I love parrot stories! Do
you all like parrot stories? Well, this one's about the old maid and the
parrot. This old maid, she had a parrot that cursed a blue streak and
knew more vulgar expressions than Mr. Kowalski.

> *She pauses, smiling at Stanley, but there is no reaction from him.*

And the only way to hush the parrot up was to put the cover back on
its cage so it would think that it was night and go back to sleep. Well,

one morning the old maid had just uncovered the parrot for the day, when who should she see coming up the front walk but the preacher! Well, she rushed back to the parrot and slipped the cover back on the cage, and then she let in the preacher.

> *Phone rings off U. R., distantly. Blanche leaps from her chair, listens.*

Oh, that must be upstairs. *(Resumes her place, and her story.)* Well, the parrot was perfectly still then—just as quiet as a mouse. But just as she was asking the preacher how much sugar he wanted in his coffee—the parrot broke the silence with: "God *damn* but that was a short day!"

> *Blanche throws back her head and laughs. Stella makes an ineffectual effort to seem amused. Stanley, who has been eating another chop, has paid no attention to story, but continues to lick his fingers.*

Apparently Mr. Kowalski was not amused.

STELLA. Mr. Kowalski is too busy making a pig of himself to think of anything else! *(To Stanley—viciously.)* Your face and your fingers are disgustingly greasy. Go and wash up and then help me clear the table.

> *A pause. Stanley looks at Stella. Suddenly, with a quick slap of his hand on chop-plate, breaks it—then with a sweep of his arm pushes his broken plate, silver, and rest of his food off table to floor. Blanche gives a frightened little gasp, turns her face away. Stella stares at Stanley, who rises and faces her across table—then she ducks her head, ashamed. Stanley crosses downstage, pushing R. chair in to table.*

STANLEY. That's how I'll clear the table. Don't ever talk that way to me. "Pig—Polack—disgusting—vulgar—greasy!" Them kind of words have been on your tongue and your sister's too much around here! What do you think you two are? A pair of queens? Remember what Huey Long said:—"Every man is a King!"—And I am the king around here, so don't you forget it!

> *Then Stanley picks up his cup, and hurls it into U. R. corner behind door.*

My place is cleared! You want me to clear your places?

He reaches for other dishes. Stella protects them. He looks at the women, stalks out onto porch, where he moves to R. end of it and faces upstage.

BLANCHE. What happened while I was bathing? What did he tell you, Stella?

STELLA. Nothing, nothing, nothing!

BLANCHE. I think he told you something about Mitch and me! I think you know why Mitch didn't come this evening, but you won't tell me!

Stella shakes her head helplessly. Blanche rises suddenly.

I'm going to call him.

STELLA. *(Rising, trying to restrain Blanche.)* I wouldn't call him, Blanche.

BLANCHE. I am, I'm going to call him on the phone.

STELLA. *(Miserably.)* I wish you wouldn't.

Crossing above Stella, Blanche takes up phone, dials. Stella goes out onto porch. Stanley does not turn to face her.

BLANCHE. I intend to be given some explanation from someone.

Orchestra plays.

STELLA. *(Reproachfully to Stanley.)* I hope you're pleased with your doings. I never had so much trouble swallowing food in my life, looking at that girl's face and the empty chair.

BLANCHE. *(At phone.)* Hello, Mr. Mitchell, please. Oh—I would like to leave a number if I may.

Stella looks in at Blanche.

Magnolia 9047.

At this point, we hear laughter, at first quiet and intimate—and soon boisterous and downright dirty, between Eunice and Steve in apartment above.

And say it's important to call. Yes, very important. Thank you.

Blanche hangs up. Stands helplessly by phone, looking about. Crosses into bedroom—faces dressing table.

STANLEY. *(Going to Stella—pulling her onto porch, turning her toward him and taking her clumsily in his arms.)* Stell, it's going to be all right after she goes and after you've had the baby. It's gonna be all right again between you and me the way it was. You remember that way that it was? Them nights we had together? God, honey, it's gonna be sweet when we can make noise in the night the way that we used to and get the colored lights going with nobody's sister behind the curtains to hear us!

Blanche crosses to head of bed, sits on it. Steve and Eunice bellow from above. Stanley chuckles, looks up.

Steve and Eunice...

Stella takes Stanley's arm and leads him back toward living room. Stanley starts to pick up some of the debris off floor. Stella goes to cabinet, gets matches to light candles. As she enters room, speaks to Stanley:

STELLA. Come on back in. *(Then, as she approaches candles with match.)* Blanche?

BLANCHE. *(Rises, moving c. between rooms.)* Yes. Oh, those pretty, pretty little candles.

Stella lights match. Blanche rushes forward and blows it out.

Oh, don't burn them, Stella!

Stanley is picking up pieces of dishes from floor.

You ought to save them for baby's birthdays. Oh, I hope candles are going to glow in his life, and I hope that his eyes are going to be like candles, like two blue candles lighted in a white cake!

STANLEY. *(Crosses to bathroom, speaks near bathroom door.)* What poetry! *(Goes into bathroom.)*

BLANCHE. *(Sitting in chair L. of table, referring to her phone call.)* I shouldn't have called him.

STELLA. *(Moving to above Blanche.)* There's lots of things could have happened.

BLANCHE. There's no excuse for it, Stella. I don't have to put up with insults. I won't be taken for granted.

Fade off music.

STANLEY. *(Coming out of bathroom, moving to c.)* Hey, Blanche, you know it's hot in here with the steam from the bathroom.

BLANCHE. *(Pounding on table and screaming at top of her voice.)* I've said I was sorry, three times! *(Turns to Stanley.)* I take hot baths for my nerves. Hydro-therapy they call it! You healthy Polack, without a nerve in your body, of course you don't know what anxiety feels like!

STANLEY. I am not a Polack. People from Poland are Poles, not Polacks. But what I am is one-hundred-per-cent American, born and raised in the greatest country on earth and proud as hell of it, so don't ever call me a Polack.

> *Phone rings. Blanche leaps up expectantly.*

BLANCHE. Oh, that's for me, I'm sure!

STANLEY. *(Moving to phone, brushes her aside.)* I'm not sure. You just keep your seat. *(Answers phone.)* H'lo. Aw, yeh, hello, Mac.

> *Blanche has followed Stanley a step or two to phone. Now she turns, almost staggers, a step R. Stella moves forward, touches Blanche's shoulder.*

BLANCHE. Oh, keep your hands off me, Stella! What is the matter with you? Why do you look at me with that pitying look?

> *She moves quickly toward cabinet and takes up liquor bottle, then comes to table and pours herself a drink, standing above table as she gulps it. Stella leans against icebox.*

STANLEY. *(Bawling at Blanche.)* Will you SHUT UP IN THERE! *(Into phone.)* We've got a noisy woman on the place. Go on, Mac. At Riley's? No, I don't wanta bowl at Riley's. I had a little trouble with Riley last week. I'm the team captain, ain't I? All right, then, we're not gonna bowl at Riley's, we're gonna bowl at the West Side or the Gala! All right, Mac, see you!

> *Stanley hangs up. Goes to Blanche at table. Stanley, reaching in his breast pocket, speaks with false amiability.*

Sister Blanche, I've got a little birthday remembrance for you.

> *He takes out envelope containing bus ticket and partly opens envelope.*

BLANCHE. Oh, have you, Stanley? I wasn't expecting any.

STANLEY. *(Handing her envelope.)* I hope you like it.

BLANCHE. *(Opening envelope and taking out ticket.)* Why, why—

why, it's a—

STANLEY. Ticket! Back to Laurel! On the Greyhound! Tuesday!

"Varsouviana" is heard through balance of scene. Blanche tries to smile. Then tries to laugh. Gives up both, turns accusingly to Stella. Suddenly, she runs above Stanley into bedroom, commencing to sob sharply. Pauses in c. of bedroom, not knowing which way to run; finally, with shaking sobs, darts into bathroom, slamming door shut. Stanley has moved to c. of living room. Stella comes to R. of him.

STELLA. You didn't need to do that.

STANLEY. Don't forget all that I took off her.

STELLA. You needn't have been so cruel to someone alone as she is.

STANLEY. Delicate piece she is.

STELLA. She is. She was. You didn't know Blanche as a girl. Nobody, nobody was tender and trusting as she was. But people like you abused her, and forced her to change.

Stanley goes up to trunk. Starts to pick up his green bowling jacket at trunk. Stella follows to below him.

Do you think you're going bowling now?

STANLEY. Sure. *(Starts to get into his jacket.)*

STELLA. You're not going bowling. *(Grabs his downstage L. arm.)* Why did you do this to her?

Stella's violent hold on his arm tears his shirt.

STANLEY. Let go of my shirt. You've torn it!

STELLA. *(Wildly.)* I want to know why! Tell me why!

STANLEY. *(Forcing Stella back a bit, handling her very roughly.)* When we first met, me and you, you thought I was common. How right you was, baby! I was common as dirt! You showed me the snapshot of the place with the columns. I pulled you down off them columns and how you loved it, having them colored lights going! And wasn't we happy together, wasn't it all okay until she showed here?

Stella pulls away from him, moves painfully to below icebox. Leans against it. He follows upstage, standing below bed, facing her, shouting:

And wasn't we happy together? Wasn't it all okay till she showed here! Hoity-toity, describing me like an ape.

A pause. He starts to put on his jacket, then turns, studies Stella. Sees she is in pain. Crosses quickly to her.

(Gently.) Hey, what is it, Stel? Did I hurt you? Whatsa matter, baby?

Clutching front door for support, Stella says weakly:

STELLA. Take me to the hospital...

He quickly supports her with his arm, and they start out.

VENDOR'S VOICE. Red hot corns—Red hot—

FADE OUT AND CURTAIN

"Varsouviana" up full through change.

SCENE 3

A while later that evening.

Rooms are dimly lighted. Blanche is seated in a tense position in armchair in bedroom, holding a drink. The sound of the "Varsouviana" is still in her ears. She wears her dressing gown. She has been drinking to escape the sense of disaster closing in on her. Fan in bedroom is spinning almost soundlessly. In the street, above, passing across from U. L. to U. R., the Flower Vendor, an old Mexican crone, calls her shining tin wares, "Flores para los muertos. Coronas. Flores." ["Flowers for the dead! Crowns! Flowers."] As she vanishes U. R., Mitch enters from same direction. He is in his work clothes. Hurries to front door of apartment and pounds on it. No answer—he repeats pounding. Fade off "Varsouviana."

BLANCHE. *(Startled.)* Who is it, please?

MITCH. *(Hoarsely.)* Me...Mitch.

BLANCHE. *(Rises.)* Mitch!—Just a minute!

Blanche darts about frantically; carrying drink, she runs into living room to hide bottle of liquor, looks about, sticks bottle and glass under L. seat. Then rushes to dressing table, by now quite beside herself, shaking and muttering. She dabs at her face—combs her hair. Mitch pounds on door, then bursts through it, stands inside dimly lighted living room. Blanche hurries to just inside living room. Mitch starts around below table, which is still set from birthday dinner, with cake and decorations.

Mitch! Y'know, I really shouldn't let you in after the treatment I have received from you this evening! So utterly uncavalier! But, hello, beautiful!

Mitch brushes past her into bedroom. Moves toward bathroom, then back upstage toward bed. He is annoyed by draught from fan.

My, my, what a cold shoulder! *(Closes door.)* And such uncouth apparel! *(Crosses to him.)* Why, you haven't even shaved! But I forgive you. I forgive you because it's such a relief to see you. You've stopped that polka tune that I had caught in my head. Have you ever had anything caught in your head?

She has moved close to him, at his R., below bed.

No, of course you haven't, you dumb angel-puss, you'd never get anything awful caught in your head!

Mitch rubs his hand across back of his neck, where he is struck by cold air from fan.

MITCH. Do we have to have that fan on?

BLANCHE. *(Crossing below him to fan, which is above dressing table on wall.)* No!

MITCH. I don't like fans.

BLANCHE. Then let's turn it off, honey. I'm not partial to them. *(Turns off fan.)* I don't know what there is to drink. I—haven't investigated. *(Starts for living room.)*

MITCH. I don't want Stan's liquor.

BLANCHE. *(Stops C.)* It isn't Stan's. Some things on the premises are actually mine! How is your mother? Isn't your mother well?

MITCH. Why?

"Varsouviana" is heard again, faintly.

BLANCHE. Something's the matter tonight, but never mind.

Hearing music, she turns away from him to back of armchair.

I won't cross-examine the witness. I'll just— *(Touches her forehead vaguely.)* —pretend I don't notice anything different about you!— that—music again…

MITCH. *(Moves a step to her L.)* What music?

BLANCHE. The polka tune they were playing when Allan—

Sound of a distant shot. "Varsouviana" music stops abruptly. Blanche, relieved:

There, now, the shot! It always stops after that. *(Listening.)* Yes, now it's stopped. *(Moves R. a step.)*

MITCH. *(Behind her.)* Are you boxed out of your mind?

BLANCHE. *(Moving into living room.)* I'll go see what I can find in the way of— *(Turns back to him.)* Oh, by the way, excuse me for not being dressed. But I'd practically given you up! Had you forgotten your invitation to supper?

She goes to cabinet, clatters among bottles, takes out clean glass.

MITCH. I wasn't going to see you any more.

BLANCHE. Wait a minute! I can't hear what you're saying, and you talk so little that when you do say something, I don't want to miss a single syllable of it!

He turns to bedroom, crosses to below bed. He puts his R. foot on bed, near head, facing upstage.

What am I looking around here for?

She wavers uncertainly above table. Holds glass she has taken from cabinet.

Oh, yes, liquor! We've had so much excitement around here this evening that I *am* boxed out of my mind!

She remembers bottle under seat, goes to it, holds it up.

Here's something! Southern Comfort! *(Standing in C. door, facing Mitch.)* What is that, I wonder?

She crosses to R. of him, carrying bottle and glass.

MITCH. If you don't know, it must belong to Stan.

BLANCHE. *(Pushing his foot off bed.)* Take your foot off the bed. It has a clean cover on it. *(Moving to L. of armchair, pouring herself a drink.)* Of course, you boys don't notice things like that. I've done so much with this place since I've been here.

MITCH. I bet you have.

BLANCHE. You saw it before I came. Well, look at it now. This room is almost—dainty! I want to keep it that way.

MITCH. *(Above her, a bit to her L.)* Aren't you leaving pretty soon now? *(Crosses D. to her.)*

BLANCHE. *(Tastes drink.)* I wonder if this stuff ought to be mixed with something? Umm. It's sweet, so sweet! It's terribly sweet! Why, it's a *liqueur*, I believe! Yes, that's what it *is*, a liqueur!

Mitch grunts. Blanche offers him glass.

I'm afraid you won't like it, but try it, and maybe you will.

MITCH. I told you already I don't want none of his liquor. And I mean it!

Blanche moves D. L., Mitch crosses to her R. and a bit above.

You ought to lay off his liquor. He says you been lapping it up all summer like a wild-cat!

BLANCHE. *(Turns to him.)* What a fantastic statement! Fantastic of him to say it, and fantastic of you to repeat it!

She goes to cabinet in living room, puts away bottle and glass. Mitch follows.

I won't descend to the level of such cheap accusations to answer them, even! What's in your mind? I see something in your eyes!

MITCH. It's dark in here!

BLANCHE. I like it dark.

Apprehensively, she moves away from him, crossing around R. end of table to C.

The dark is comforting to me.

MITCH. I don't think I ever seen you in the light. That's a fact!

He goes to light switch on pillar u. r., turns on overhead light.

BLANCHE. Is it?

She flees from Mitch and the light into bedroom.

MITCH. *(Following, keeping close behind her.)* I've never seen you in the afternoon.

BLANCHE. *(Below dressing table.)* Whose fault is that?

MITCH. *(Following.)* You never want to go out in the afternoon.

BLANCHE. *(Facing away from him, near bathroom door.)* Why, Mitch, you're at the plant in the afternoon!

MITCH. *(Behind her.)* Not Sunday afternoon. You never want to go out till after six, and then it's always some place that's not lighted much.

BLANCHE. There is some obscure meaning in this, but I fail to catch it.

MITCH. *(Overlapping her speech; turns her to him.)* What it means is, I've never had a real good look at you, Blanche.

He leaves her, moves toward bracket which holds paper lantern.

Let's turn on the light here! *(Picks up dressing-table chair, shoves it upstage.)*

BLANCHE. *(Fearfully.)* Light? Which light? What for?

MITCH. This one, with the paper thing on it!

He rips paper lantern off bulb, tosses lantern to floor in front of Blanche. She drops to her knees with a little cry, trying to rescue lantern.

BLANCHE. What did you do that for?

MITCH. So I can take a look at you, good and plain!

BLANCHE. Of course you don't really mean to be insulting!

MITCH. No, just realistic.

BLANCHE. I don't want realism. I want—magic!

MITCH. *(Laughing.)* Magic!

BLANCHE. *(Still on her knees.)* Yes, yes, magic! I try to give that to people. I do misrepresent things to them. I don't tell the truth, I tell what *ought* to be truth. And if that's a sin, then let me be damned for it! *Don't turn the light on!*

> *Mitch snaps light on, comes back, pulls Blanche to her feet, shoves her back against dressing table, pushing her face into harsh glare of the naked bulb.*

MITCH. *(Slowly and bitterly.)* I don't mind you being older than what I thought. But all the rest of it—

> *Pause—then he shouts:*

CHRIST!

> *He drops her arms and steps back a bit away from her.*

That pitch about your ideals being so old-fashioned, and all the malarkey that you've been dishing out all summer. Oh, I knew you weren't sixteen anymore. But I was a fool enough to believe you were straight.

BLANCHE. *(Leaning against dressing table, facing him.)* Who told you I wasn't—"straight"? My loving brother-in-law. And you believed him.

MITCH. *(A step toward her.)* No! I called him a liar at first. And then I checked on the story. First I asked our supply-man who travels through Laurel. And then I talked directly over long distance to this merchant.

BLANCHE. Who is this merchant?

MITCH. Kiefaber.

BLANCHE. The merchant Kiefaber of Laurel! I know the man. He whistled at me. I put him in his place. So now for revenge, he makes up stories about me.

> *Next few speeches overlap in rapidity with which they are spoken.*

MITCH. Three people, Kiefaber, Stanley, and Shaw, swore to them!

BLANCHE. *(On "Kiefaber.")* Rub-a-dub-dub, three men in a tub!—a such a filthy tub!

MITCH. *(On "tub"—the first time.)* Didn't you stay at a hotel called the Flamingo?

103

BLANCHE. Flamingo? No! Tarantula was the name of it! I stayed at a hotel called the Tarantula Arms!

MITCH. *(Stupidly.)* Tarantula Arms?

BLANCHE. Yes, a big spider! That's where I brought my victims.

Pause.

Yes, I had many intimacies with strangers. After the death of Allan—intimacies with strangers was all I seemed able to fill my empty heart with.

Pause.

I think it was panic—just panic that drove me from one to another, searching for some protection—in the most unlikely places! Even, at last, in a seventeen-year-old boy— *(To Mitch.)* But somebody wrote the superintendent, "This woman is morally unfit for her position!" True? Yes, I suppose—unfit somehow—anyway... So I came here. There was nowhere else I could go. I was played out. You know what played out means? My youth was suddenly gone up the water-spout and I—met you. You said you needed somebody. Well, I needed somebody, too. I thanked God for you, because you seemed to be gentle—a cleft in the rock of the world that I could hide in!

Blanche crosses to him, touches him. He draws back to below bed. She crosses slowly into living room, speaking as she walks, moves to above L. end of table.

But I suppose I was asking, hoping too much!

Outside, D. R., Mexican Vendor Woman is heard approaching, and sound of her call, "Flores para los muertos," is heard—indistinctly at first, then more clearly.

Kiefaber, Stanley, and Shaw tied an old tin can to the tail of the kite. *(Crosses to corner of table.)*

MITCH. You lied to me, Blanche. *(Crosses in to her.)*

BLANCHE. *(Turns on him.)* Don't say I lied to you.

MITCH. Lies, lies, inside and out, all lies.

BLANCHE. Never inside. I didn't lie in my heart. I was true as God in my heart to all of you—*always*—always!

The Mexican woman has appeared by this time, carrying

her tin flowers, coming onto porch. As Blanche says the first "always" in the speech immediately preceding, the Mexican woman mutters "Flores!" on porch. Blanche, hearing her:

What?

MEXICAN WOMAN. Flores...

BLANCHE. Oh, somebody outside...

She starts for door. "Varsouviana" heard. Blanche opens it, stares at Mexican woman.

MEXICAN WOMAN. *(Immediately outside front door.)* Flores. Flores para los muertos?

BLANCHE. *(Frightened.)* No, no! Not now! Not now!

She darts back into apartment, slamming door.

MEXICAN WOMAN. *(Turning away, starting u. r. through street.)* Flores para los muertos.

BLANCHE. *(Moving slowly to above table.)* I lived in a house where dying old women remembered their dead men...

MEXICAN WOMAN. *(In street, moving toward u. l. exit.)* Flores. Flores para los muertos...

BLANCHE. *(As if to herself.)* Crumble and fade—regrets—recriminations...

MEXICAN WOMAN. Coronas.

BLANCHE. "If you'd done this it wouldn't have cost me that!" *(Moving quickly to below couch.)* Legacies!

MEXICAN WOMAN. Coronas para los muertos. Coronas...

BLANCHE. And other things, such as blood-stained pillowslips—"Her linen needs changing"—"Yes, Mother. But couldn't we get a colored girl to do it?"—No, we couldn't of course—Everything gone but—

MEXICAN WOMAN. Flores...

BLANCHE. Death.

MEXICAN WOMAN. Flores para los muertos.

BLANCHE. I used to sit here and she used to sit over there and death was as close as you are.

MEXICAN WOMAN. Coronas.

BLANCHE. We didn't dare even admit we had ever heard of it.

MEXICAN WOMAN. Coronas para los muertos...

BLANCHE. Death.

MEXICAN WOMAN. Flores...

BLANCHE. The opposite is Desire.

MEXICAN WOMAN. *(Faintly.)* Flores...

BLANCHE. So do you wonder? How could you possibly wonder?

MEXICAN WOMAN. *(Very faintly—almost off U. L.)* Coronas...

BLANCHE. *(Sits in chair L. of table.)* Not far from Belle Reve, before we had lost Belle Reve, was a camp where they trained young soldiers. On Saturday nights they would go into town and get drunk. And on the way back they would stagger onto my lawn and call, "Blanche! Blanche!"—The deaf old lady remaining suspected nothing. But sometimes I slipped outside to answer their calls... Later the paddy-wagon would gather them up like daisies...the long way home...

> *On "answer their calls" she has arisen and gone D. R. below table. Fade off "Varsouviana." Mitch crosses quickly to behind Blanche, places his arms about her waist and turns her about. At first she takes him, passionately, then pushes him away. He seizes her roughly—grasping a few strands of her hair in his L. hand.*

What do you want?

MITCH. *(Fumbling to embrace her.)* What I been missing all summer.

BLANCHE. Then marry me, Mitch!

MITCH. No! You're not clean enough to bring in the house with my mother.

BLANCHE. *(Loudly.)* Go away then.

> *He stares at her, then starts backing up around table toward door.*

Get out of here quick before I start screaming fire!

He scrambles to get out door. She follows him, shouting:

Get out of here quick before I start screaming fire!

He hurries out door and off U. R. *Blanche stands in doorway screaming:*

Fire! Fire! Fire!

FADE OUT AND CURTAIN

Orchestra plays through change. "Good Night Ladies" commences under other music and miked applause.

SCENE 4

A few hours later, same night.

Blanche has been drinking fairly steadily since preceding scene. She has opened her wardrobe trunk and thrown a goodly amount of her fancy clothing around the apartment. Beds, armchair, trunk are covered with finery. Jewel box is in lid of trunk. A bottle stands mutely on dressing table. [This is the break-away bottle used late in the scene.] Blanche is standing before dressing table, glass in hand. She is dressed in a somewhat soiled and crumpled white satin evening gown and a pair of scuffed slippers. She wears the rhinestone tiara in her disarranged hair. A mood of hysterical exhilaration has possessed her, and she fancies she hears applause and favorable comments of her old friends at a party at Belle Reve. Applause and chatter effect on mike from R., *dying away as curtain rises.*

BLANCHE. How about taking a swim, a moonlight swim at the old rock quarry? If anyone's sober enough to drive a car! Best way in the world to stop your head buzzing! Only you've got to be careful to dive where the deep pool is, if you don't come up till tomorrow.

Stanley enters from D. R., *comes into apartment. He is still wearing his torn shirt and has returned from hospital. Carries a large paper bag, in which are a bottle of beer, a bottle of liquor, a bottle opener, and some pretzel sticks. Door to apartment is open. He leaves it open, puts paper bag down on table, goes to icebox. Gets a glass from cabinet. Then sees Blanche. Stanley grasps the situation. "Good Night Ladies" is heard as Blanche murmurs to her group of spectral admirers:*

Oh, my goodness! They're playing "Good Night Ladies." May I rest my weary head on your shoulder? It's so comforting…

> *She stands u. c. in bedroom, laying her head against her hand. Music dies out.*

STANLEY. Hiyah, Blanche!

BLANCHE. *(Coming in to c., speaks to him.)* How is my sister?

STANLEY. *(At table, puts down glass.)* She is doing okay.

BLANCHE. And how is the baby?

STANLEY. *(Grinning amiably.)* The baby won't come before morning, so they told me to go home and get a little shut-eye. *(Takes bottles out of bag, puts them on table.)*

BLANCHE. *(A step into living room.)* Does that mean we are to be alone in here?

STANLEY. *(Looks at Blanche, who crosses to dresser.)* Yep. Just me and you, Blanche. What've you got those fine feathers on for?

BLANCHE. *(In bedroom.)* Oh, that's right. You left before my wire came.

STANLEY. You got a wire?

BLANCHE. I received a telegram from an old admirer of mine.

STANLEY. Anything good?

BLANCHE. I think so. An invitation.

STANLEY. What to?

> *Blanche crosses c. to below trunk.*

BLANCHE. A cruise on the Caribbean on a yacht!

STANLEY. Well, well. What do you know!

BLANCHE. I have never been so surprised in my life.

STANLEY. I guess not.

BLANCHE. It came like a bolt from the blue!

STANLEY. Who did you say it was from?

BLANCHE. An old beau of mine.

Stanley picks up liquor bottle and crosses a step toward her.

STANLEY. The one that gave you the white fox-pieces?

BLANCHE. Mr. Shep Huntleigh. I wore his ATO pin my last year at college. I hadn't seen him again until last Christmas. I ran into him on Biscayne Boulevard. Then—just now—this wire—inviting me to a cruise of the Caribbean! The problem is clothes! I tore into my trunk to see what I have that's suitable for the tropics! *(Crosses to trunk.)*

STANLEY. And come up with that—gorgeous—diamond—tiara?

BLANCHE. This old relic! It's only rhinestones.

STANLEY. Gosh. I thought it was Tiffany's diamonds.

BLANCHE. *(In c.)* Well, anyhow, I shall be entertained in style.

STANLEY. *(Puts liquor bottle on table.)* It goes to show you, you never know what is coming.

BLANCHE. Just when I thought my luck had begun to fail me—

STANLEY. Into the picture pops this Miami millionaire.

BLANCHE. This man is not from Miami. This man is from Dallas.

STANLEY. *(Crossing below Blanche into bedroom, taking off shirt.)* This man is from Dallas?

BLANCHE. Yes, this man is from Dallas, where gold spouts out of the ground!

STANLEY. *(Tossing shirt on bureau.)* Well, just so he's from somewhere!

BLANCHE. *(Moving vaguely below trunk.)* Close the curtains before you undress any further.

STANLEY. *(Amiably.)* This is all I'm going to undress right now.

He crosses below her to icebox. She retires to bedroom, draping her torn veil about her, casting side-long glances at herself in mirror, L.

Seen a bottle-opener?

He is peering into cabinet.

I used to have a cousin could open a beer-bottle with his teeth.

He comes to table, sits on it, gets out beer bottle, prepares to open it.

That was his only accomplishment, all he could do—he was just a human bottle-opener. *(Sits above table.)* And then, one time, at a wedding party, *(Finds opener in bag.)* he broke his front teeth off! After that, he was so ashamed of himself he used t' sneak out of the house when company came…

Stanley opens beer bottle. Foam gushes forth. Stanley laughs happily, holding up bottle, letting beer cascade over his arms and person.

Rain from heaven! *(Drinks.)* What'ya say, Blanche? *(Rises, starts L. into bedroom, with beer bottle.)* Shall we bury the hatchet and make it a loving-cup?

Blanche, terrified, darts below him into living room.

BLANCHE. No, thank you.

STANLEY. *(Putting beer bottle in armchair.)* Aw, get with it, Blanche!

BLANCHE. *(At R. side of door C.)* What are you doing in here?

Sitting on bed, Stanley pulls footlocker out from beneath bed, gets out coat of red silk pajamas.

STANLEY. Here's something I always break out on special occasions like this. The silk pyjamas I wore on my wedding night! *(Grabs them up, closes locker, kicks it under bed.)*

BLANCHE. Oh.

STANLEY. And when the telephone rings, and they say, "You've got a son!" I'll tear this off and wave it like a flag!

Blanche mills up and downstage R. of C. He waves pajama coat aloft and rises.

I guess we are both entitled to put on the dog!

He wipes his face on pajama coat, throws it on dressing table. Comes into living room. She moves upstage to avoid him.

You having an oil millionaire, and me having a baby! *(Goes to above table.)*

Blanche, who has drawn back at C. to let him pass below her, stands below pillar, holding curtain between them, faces L.

BLANCHE. When I think of how divine it is going to be to have such a thing as privacy once more—I could weep with joy!

STANLEY. *(Above table; eating pretzel sticks from paper bag.)* This millionaire from Dallas is not going to interfere with your privacy any?

BLANCHE. *(In doorway.)* It won't be the sort of thing you have in mind. This man is a gentleman, and he respects me. *(Improvising feverishly.)* What he wants is my companionship. Having great wealth sometimes makes people lonely! A cultivated woman, a woman of intelligence and breeding, can enrich a man's life immeasurably! I have those things to offer, and time doesn't take them away. Physical beauty is passing, a transitory possession. But beauty of the mind and richness of the spirit and tenderness of the heart—and I have all those things!—aren't taken away, but grow! Increase with the years! How strange that I should be called a destitute woman! When I have all of these treasures locked in my heart. I think of myself as a very, very rich woman! But I have been foolish—casting my pearls before—

STANLEY. Swine, huh?

BLANCHE. *(Protecting herself with curtain at C.)* Yes, swine! Swine! And I'm thinking not only of you, but of your friend, Mr. Mitchell. He came to see me tonight. He dared to come here in his work-clothes! And to repeat slander to me, vicious stories that he had gotten from you!—I gave him his walking papers!

STANLEY. You did, huh?

BLANCHE. *(At C. R. of pillar, dropping curtain.)* But then he came back. He returned with a box of roses to beg my forgiveness. He implored my forgiveness. But some things are not forgivable. Deliberate cruelty is not forgivable.

Stanley rises—crosses nearer to her.

It is the one unforgivable thing in my opinion and it is the one thing of which I have never, never been guilty. And so I told him, I said to him, Thank you, but it was foolish of me to think that we could ever adapt ourselves to each other. Our ways of life are too different.

Stanley leans on back of L. chair.

Our attitudes and our backgrounds are incompatible. We have to be realistic about such things. So, farewell, my friend! And let there be no hard feeling...

STANLEY. Was this before or after the telegram came from Texas?

BLANCHE. *(Moving D. L. in living room, halts abruptly.)* What telegram? *(Half turns to Stanley, then moves on D. L.)* No! No, after! As a matter of fact, the wire came just as—

Stanley, cutting in, following her, pushes her down L. seat.

STANLEY. As a matter of fact, there wasn't no wire at all!

BLANCHE. *(Sitting on seat.)* Oh, oh!

STANLEY. There isn't no millionaire, and Mitch didn't come back here with no roses, because I know where he is!

BLANCHE. Oh!

STANLEY. There isn't a damn thing but imagination, and lies, and conceit and tricks! *(Clutches train of her dress.)* And look at yourself! *(Throws train at her.)* Take a look at yourself in that worn-out Mardi Gras outfit, rented for fifty cents from some rag-picker! *(Snaps his fingers.)* And with that crazy crown on! *(Sweeps it off her head, tosses it upstage.)* What kind of a queen do you think you are?

BLANCHE. *(Fleeing to R. of table.)* Oh, God...

STANLEY. *(Following her.)* I've been on to you from the start.

Blanche flees to below table, then as he follows her she goes above table to C., cowering. Stanley stands at R. end of table, glaring at her.

Not once did you pull any wool over this boy's eyes!

Blanche retreats into bedroom. Stanley follows to C.

You come in here and sprinkle the place with powder and spray perfume, and cover the light bulb with a paper lantern, and lo and behold the place has turned into Egypt and you are Queen of the Nile!

Blanche retreats to corner of bathroom door. Stanley follows, relentlessly.

Sitting on your throne, and swilling down my liquor! I say—*Ha! Ha!*

He clutches her firmly, as she nearly faints in his grasp.

Do you hear me? *Ha-ha-ha!*

> *Stanley pushes her aside. He picks up his pajama coat from dressing table and goes into bathroom, slamming door. Scream is heard off, U. L. Sound of excited murmuring in street, and from café U. R. Blanche runs to phone, terrified at sounds from outside. As she dials, following occurs in street: A woman laughs insanely and runs into street from U. L. with a purse. A man in a tuxedo follows, protesting. Woman strikes him. He falls. Babel offstage increases. Another man rushes on from U. R., attacks first man from behind. Sound of police whistles and a siren in the distance, groans from the felled man as his assailants vanish R. and L. Blanche, during this, at phone:*

BLANCHE. Operator, operator! Give me long distance, please.—I want to get in touch with Mr. Shep Huntleigh of Dallas. He's so well-known he doesn't require any address. Just ask anybody who—Wait!! No, I couldn't find it right now—please understand—I—No! No!—Wait! I can't! I can't!

> *She puts down phone, trembling. A man runs in from U. R., followed by three thugs who attack him D. R., where they are joined by another man, C. More police whistles. Men vanish out D. R., and there is an excited murmur of their voices. Wounded man staggers off U. R. Blanche, frightened, goes to her trunk, takes up jewel box and a couple of gowns, goes out onto porch, where she comes face to face with the muggers, just before they go out D. R. She rushes back into apartment, leaving door open. Goes once more to phone, kneels beside it, clutching her possessions.*

Operator! Operator! Never mind long distance. Get Western Union. There isn't time to be—Western—Western Union!

> *Pause.*

Union? Yes! I want to—Take down this message: "In desperate, desperate circumstances! Help me! Caught in a trap! Caught in—" *(Hears a sound from bathroom door.)* Oh!

113

Stanley emerges from bathroom. He has put out bathroom light. He is dressed in his red silk pajamas. He grins at Blanche, who rises, backs away from phone into living room. He advances to phone, which is clicking, receiver off hook. Puts receiver back on hook.

STANLEY. You left the phone off the hook.

Stanley picks up beer bottle from armchair. Passes below Blanche to U. R. corner. Puts bottle on cabinet. Closes the door deliberately.

BLANCHE. *(Starting after him.)* Let me get out—let me get by you!

STANLEY. Get by me? Sure. Go ahead.

BLANCHE. *(Indicating a place somewhere L.)* You—you stand over there!

STANLEY. *(Pushing upper chair under table.)* You got plenty of room to walk by me now.

BLANCHE. Not with you there! But I've got to get out somehow!

She runs into bedroom frantically, pulling drapes closed. Crosses to below dressing table.

STANLEY. *(Following, pushing drapes open.)* You think I'll interfere with you? *(Softly.)* Come to think of it—maybe you wouldn't be bad to—interfere with…

BLANCHE. *(Below dressing table.)* Stay back! Don't you come toward me another step or I'll—

STANLEY. What?

BLANCHE. Some awful thing will happen! It will!

STANLEY. *(Closing in slowly.)* What are you putting on now?

BLANCHE. I warn you, don't! I'm in danger!

As she continues, she grabs bottle up from dressing table, smashes it, holds broken end of it toward him.

STANLEY. What did you do that for?

BLANCHE. So I could twist the broken end in your face!

STANLEY. I bet you would do that!

BLANCHE. I would! I will if—

STANLEY. Oh, you want some rough-house! All right, let's have some rough-house!

He springs toward her. She cries out. He seizes her hand holding bottle, twists it behind her.

Tiger—tiger! Drop the bottle-top! Drop it!

She drops bottle-top. He bends her to his will, picks her up in his arms.

We've had this date with each other from the beginning!

He starts toward bed with her.

QUICK FADE OUT AND CURTAIN

Orchestra plays through change.

SCENE 5

Some days later.

Music fades off at rise. Some of Blanche's slips are on bed, one on back of armchair. The dress she will wear is draped over back of dressing-table chair. Her jacket is on bed. Stella is back from the hospital and has Blanche's suitcase open on dressing-table chair, which faces upstage. She is packing Blanche's things, standing below bed, folding slips, which she puts in suitcase which she then closes. Blanche's trunk is closed, locked. Curtains between rooms are closed. In living room another poker game is in progress. Stanley is seated above table, Mitch at his R., Steve below table, and Pablo at L. Blanche's jewel box is lying on armchair. Stella has been crying as she arranges slips. Eunice comes down from above, carrying dish full of grapes and other fruit. When she enters living room, there is an outburst from poker game. Eunice closes front door behind her. Stella comes to above armchair, picks up slip from back of chair, starts to fold it.

115

STANLEY. Drew to an inside straight and made it, by God!

PABLO. *(Rising.)* Maldita sea tu suerto!

STANLEY. Put it in English, grease-ball!

PABLO. I am cursing your rutting luck!

STANLEY. *(To Mitch, prodigiously elated.)* You know what luck is? Luck is believing you're lucky. Take at Salerno. I believed I was lucky. I figured that four out of five would not come through, but I would…and I did. I put that down as a rule. To hold a front position in this rat race you've got to believe you're lucky.

MITCH. *(Furiously.)* You…you…you…brag…brag…bull…bull…

> *He turns away from game, faces front and rests his chin on arm on back of his chair.*

STANLEY. *(To others, astonished.)* What's the matter with him?

EUNICE. *(Above poker table, walking to c. and l.)* I always did say that men were callous things with no feelings, but this does beat anything. Making pigs of yourselves. *(Goes through curtains into bedroom.)*

STANLEY. What's the matter with her? Come on, let's play.

> *Game resumes in silence. As Eunice enters bedroom, she crosses around Stella to backless chair in D. R. corner.*

STELLA. How's my baby? Is he demanding his supper?

EUNICE. *(Putting bowl of grapes on backless chair, backing L. a few steps.)* Sleepin' like a little angel. Brought you some grapes.

> *Stella moves downstage at L. of Eunice, leaving slip on back of armchair.*

STELLA. Bless him. I just ache when I'm not in the same room with him.

EUNICE. You better leave him right there till you know what gets settled. Where is she?

STELLA. Bathing.

EUNICE. How is she?

STELLA. She wouldn't eat anything, but asked for a drink.

EUNICE. What did you tell her?

STELLA. I just told her we made arrangements for her to rest in the country. She's got it mixed up in her mind with Shep Huntleigh.

BLANCHE. *(Opens bathroom door, calls out.)* Stella!

Eunice moves upstage to L. of armchair.

STELLA. Yes, Blanche?

BLANCHE. If anyone calls while I'm bathing, take the number and tell him I'll call right back.

STELLA. Yes.

BLANCHE. *(With difficulty in being coherent.)* And, Stella—that cool yellow silk—the boucle—see if it's crushed. If it's not too crushed I'll wear it and on the lapel that silver and turquoise pin in the shape of a sea-horse. You will find them in the heart-shaped box I keep my accessories in. And, oh, Stella—try to locate that bunch of artificial— *(Long difficult effort to remember name of flower.)* violets in that box, too, to pin with the sea-horse on the lapel of the jacket.

Blanche closes door. Stella turns to Eunice, going to jewel box in armchair, takes up ribbons, a discarded domino, etc.

STELLA. I just don't know if I did the right thing!

She sits dejectedly on arm of chair, letting baubles from jewel box spill through her fingers.

EUNICE. *(Moving near Stella.)* What else could you do?

STELLA. I couldn't believe her story and go on living with Stanley!

She breaks, turns to Eunice, who takes her in her arms.

EUNICE. *(Holding Stella close.)* Don't you ever believe it. You've got to keep on goin', honey. No matter what happens, we've all got to keep on going.

BLANCHE. *(Opening door, peeking out of bathroom.)* Stella, is the coast clear?

STELLA. Yes, Blanche. *(Rises, to Eunice.)* Tell her how well she's looking.

BLANCHE. *(Stepping out of bathroom, carrying hairbrush.)* Please close the curtains before I come out. *(Closes bathroom door.)*

STELLA. *(Going to curtains.)* They're closed.

Stella shows Blanche that they are.

STANLEY. *(Speaking low, at the game.)* Hey, Mitch.

Dialogue in the bedroom does not wait on conversation over the poker game. Pablo makes a characteristic comment. Blanche is in her robe. She brushes her hair as she stands U. L. There is a tragic radiance about her.

BLANCHE. *(Speaking with a faintly hysterical vivacity.)* I have just washed my hair.

STELLA. Did you?

BLANCHE. I'm not sure I got the soap out.

EUNICE. Such fine hair!

BLANCHE. *(Accepting the compliment.)* It's a problem. Didn't I get a call?

STELLA. Who from, Blanche?

BLANCHE. *(Moving to between Stella and Eunice.)* Shep Huntleigh…

STELLA. Why, not yet, honey!

BLANCHE. How strange! I—

At sound of Blanche's voice, Mitch's arm has sagged and his gaze is dissolved into space. Stanley barks at him:

STANLEY. Hey, Mitch! Come to!

Mitch returns to game. The sound of this new voice shocks Blanche. She makes a little gesture, forming Mitch's name with her lips, questioningly. Stella nods and looks quickly away. Blanche stands below bed, looking perplexed. She glances from Stella to Eunice. Stella glances away.

BLANCHE. *(With sudden hysteria.)* What's happened here? I want an explanation of what's going on here? *(Moves downstage L. below dressing table.)*

STELLA. *(Agonizingly.)* Hush! Hush!

EUNICE. Hush! Hush! Honey!

STELLA. Please, Blanche.

BLANCHE. Why are you two looking at me like that? Is something wrong with me?

EUNICE. *(Moving to L. of Stella.)* You look wonderful, Blanche. Don't she look wonderful?

STELLA. Yes.

> *Blanche is removing her robe below dressing table.*

EUNICE. I understand you're going on a trip.

STELLA. Yes, Blanche *is*. She's going on a vacation.

EUNICE. I'm green with envy.

BLANCHE. *(Exasperated, dropping her bathrobe on arm of dressing-table chair.)* Help me, you two! Help me get dressed!

STELLA. *(Taking up Blanche's dress from back of dressing-table chair and going to her with it.)* Is this what you want?

BLANCHE. *(Taking dress, getting into it.)* Yes, it will do! I'm anxious to get out of here. This place is a trap!

EUNICE. *(Going to bed, picking up Blanche's violet-colored jacket.)* Such a pretty blue jacket. *(Holds it up.)*

> *Stella helps Blanche into dress, standing behind her.*

STELLA. It's lilac-colored.

EUNICE. I'm color-blind as a bat.

BLANCHE. *(Spying grapes, crossing to backless chair, picks up a grape.)* Are these grapes washed?

> *Chimes. Eunice starts D. L. Puts jacket on bed.*

EUNICE. Huh?

BLANCHE. *(Below armchair.)* Washed, I said, are they washed?

EUNICE. *(Just above Stella.)* Why, they're from the French Market.

BLANCHE. That doesn't mean they've been washed. *(Listens to chimes.)* Ah, those cathedral bells, they're the only clean thing in the Quarter. Well, I'm going now. *(Crosses U. to below bed.)* I'm ready to go. *(Puts on jacket.)*

EUNICE. *(Whispering to Stella.)* She's going to walk out before they get here.

> *Stella, crossing quickly below Blanche, stands at Blanche's R., and just inside—at L.—of C. chair.*

STELLA. Wait, Blanche.

BLANCHE. *(Looking toward living room.)* I don't want to pass in front of those men.

EUNICE. *(Below dressing table.)* Then wait till the game breaks up.

STELLA. Yes—sit down and…

BLANCHE. *(Suddenly listening, as she puts on hood, to a far-away sound, inhaling a far-off odor.)* I can smell the sea-air. My element is the earth—but it should have been the water—water—the blessedest thing that God created in those seven days. The rest of my days I'm going to spend on the sea.

>*Fade off chimes.*

And when I die, I'm going to die on the sea. You know what I shall die of? I shall die of eating an unwashed grape. One day out on the ocean I will die—with my hand in the hand of some nice-looking ship's doctor, a very young one with a small blond moustache and a big silver watch. "Poor lady,"

>*Chimes.*

they'll say, "The quinine did her no good. That unwashed grape has transported her soul to heaven." *(Moves D.S. to below armchair.)* And I'll be buried at sea sewn up in a clean white sack and dropped overboard at noon—in the blaze of summer—and into an ocean as blue as—the blue of my first lover's eyes!

>*Stella comes to Blanche, takes her in her arms. A Strange Man appears on porch and rings doorbell. He is followed by a Strange Woman, severely dressed in a dark, tailored suit and carrying a small black, professional-looking bag. Chimes fade away as doorbell sounds.*

EUNICE. *(To Stella, when doorbell rings.)* That must be them.

>*Stanley rises, goes to door to answer bell. A low exchange between him and Strange Man. Stanley says: "Doctor?" The Strange Man, "Yes." Stanley nods, says: "Just a minute." Turns back into living room.*

BLANCHE. *(On hearing bell.)* What is it?

EUNICE. *(Covering.)* Excuse me while I see who's at the door. *(Starts through curtains.)*

STELLA. Yes.

Eunice comes into living room, meets Stanley above table. Stanley tells her the doctor has arrived. Eunice takes a quick glance onto porch.

BLANCHE. *(Tensely, going to dressing table.)* I wonder if it's for me?

Stella goes to above armchair, faces upstage. Eunice returns to bedroom, pats Stella's arm—then crosses above Stella to R. of Blanche. She speaks brightly to Blanche.

EUNICE. Someone is calling for Blanche.

BLANCHE. *(Taking Eunice's hand.)* It *is* for me, then! Is it the gentleman I was expecting from Dallas?

EUNICE. *(Looks at Stella.)* I think it is, Blanche.

BLANCHE. *(Turning to dressing table.)* I'm not quite ready.

STELLA. Ask him to wait outside.

BLANCHE. I...

Eunice returns to living room, nods to Stanley. Stanley turns to Strange Man on porch and says, "She'll be here in a minute." Strange Man nods, turns to Strange Woman, and tells her same thing.

STELLA. *(Crossing to behind Blanche—taking slip from back of armchair to suitcase.)* Everything packed?

BLANCHE. My silver toilet articles are still out.

STELLA. Ah!

She hurries to below dressing table, opens suitcase, gathers up articles, packs them quickly—together with slip.

EUNICE. *(Returning to below R. end of bed.)* They're waiting in front of the house.

BLANCHE. They? Who's "they"?

EUNICE. There's a lady with him.

BLANCHE. I wonder who this "lady" could be!

She looks at Stella, who averts her eyes. Turns to Eunice.

How is she dressed?

EUNICE. Just—just a sort of—plain-tailored outfit.

Stella closes suitcase, stays above dressing-table chair.

BLANCHE. Possibly she's—

Her voice dies out nervously. Stanley has moved L. in living room and is standing facing drawn curtains.

STELLA. Shall we go, Blanche? *(Takes up suitcase.)*

BLANCHE. Yes.

Eunice opens curtains. Blanche stares at Stanley. Turns to Stella.

Must we go through that room?

Stanley steps downstage to R. of L. seat.

STELLA. I will go with you.

BLANCHE. *(To Stella.)* How do I look? *(Turns to Eunice.)*

STELLA. Lovely.

EUNICE. *(Echoing.)* Lovely.

Blanche starts into living room, Stella following. Stella hands suitcase to Eunice, who follows.

BLANCHE. *(Crossing above table to door.)* Please don't get up. I'm only passing through.

Stella follows closely behind Blanche, and Eunice comes to a position close behind Stella. Blanche steps onto porch and stares at Strange Man, who turns to her with a kindly look. Blanche, retreating slowly, looks at Stella. Back to Man.

You are not the gentleman I was expecting.

Stella turns quickly into Eunice's arms. Stanley steps to behind Eunice, kisses Stella's hand.

That man isn't Shep Huntleigh!

She runs into bedroom, darts behind head of bed.

STANLEY. *(As Blanche passes him.)* Did you forget something?

Strange Man enters room of commotion—motions Strange Woman, who also enters. Stella starts for Blanche—Eunice holds her back.

BLANCHE. *(Shrilly.)* Yes, yes, I forgot something!

Strange Man has stepped into room. Stands by door. Strange Woman crosses through living room. Stella starts after her. Stanley stops Stella gently, and Eunice draws Stella back into her arms. Mitch rises. Strange Woman puts her bag on bed, stands facing Blanche, who cowers behind screen at head of bed. Woman speaks in a voice as bold and toneless as a fire-bell.

STRANGE WOMAN. Hello, Blanche!

STANLEY. *(Turning to bedroom, standing below trunk.)* She says she forgot something.

STRANGE WOMAN. That's all right.

STANLEY. What did you forget, Blanche?

BLANCHE. *(Coming D. at upstage end of dresser.)* I—I—

STRANGE WOMAN. It don't matter. We can pick it up later.

STANLEY. Sure. We can send it along with the trunk. *(Taps Blanche's closed trunk.)*

BLANCHE. *(Slowly retreating in panic to D. C.)* I don't know you! I don't know you! I want to be—left alone—please! *(Crosses D. L.)*

STRANGE WOMAN. *(Advancing.)* Now, Blanche!

VOICES. *(Off L., upstage, echoing and reechoing.)* Now, Blanche! Now, Blanche! Now, Blanche!

STANLEY. *(Crossing below Strange Woman to R. of dressing table.)* Now, Blanche—you left nothing here but spilt talcum and old empty perfume bottles, unless it's the paper lantern you want to take with you. *(Reaches up for lantern.)* You want the lantern?

> *He tears lantern off light bulb and throws it down on dressing table. Blanche cries out. Stanley turns away to C. door. Blanche darts U. C. with lantern. Strange Woman seizes Blanche's arm and forces her to the floor, her head toward footlights, lying between the dressing table and armchair. Following occurs almost simultaneously:*

> *Strange Man crosses D.S. R.—then to C.—and U. through arch to bedroom.*

STELLA. *(Rushing onto porch.)* Oh, my God, Eunice, help me! Don't let them hurt her! Oh, God! Oh, please, God, don't hurt her! What are they doing to her! What are they doing?

STANLEY. *(Sotto voce.)* Hey! Hey! Doctor, you'd better go in.

123

Eunice, following, to R. of Stella, puts down grip between foot of stairs and D. R. pillar.

EUNICE. No, honey, no, no, honey. Stay here. Don't go back in there. *(Holds Stella.)* Stay with me and don't look.

STELLA. *(Moving U. a couple of steps on circular stair.)* What have I done to my sister! Oh, God, what have I done to my sister!

EUNICE. *(Moving with Stella—still holding her.)* You done the right thing, the only thing you could do. She couldn't stay here, there wasn't no other place for her to go.

During this, Mitch has started below table, around it to U. C., where he rushes Stanley. Steve sees Mitch go for Stanley.

MITCH. You! You done this, all a your God-damn rutting with things you—

The men grapple. Pablo and Steve pull Mitch off Stanley and push him down in chair at R. of table, where he collapses, head in arms, sobbing. Strange Man has passed below them into bedroom, kneels beside prostrate form of Blanche, at her R.—the Strange Woman kneeling at Blanche's L., holding Blanche's hands firmly behind her back.

STRANGE WOMAN. *(Pinioning Blanche's arms.)* These fingernails will have to be trimmed. Jacket, Doctor?

STRANGE MAN. Not unless necessary.

Stanley is standing U. C., Pablo to his R., and Steve above Mitch, comforting him. The Strange Man, leaning close to Blanche, lifting her eyelids:

Miss DuBois—

BLANCHE. *(Turns to him, pleadingly.)* Please.

STRANGE MAN. *(To Strange Woman.)* It won't be necessary.

BLANCHE. *(Faintly.)* Ask her to let go of me.

STRANGE MAN. *(To Strange Woman.)* Yes—let go.

Strange Woman releases Blanche and rises. Steps D.S. L. a bit. Strange Man helps Blanche to her feet. He takes off his hat. She looks at him, wavering at first, then smiling, as she would at a new beau. She looks triumphantly at Strange Woman, then back to Strange Man with a radiant smile.

Stanley returns to his place at table, sits. Blanche crosses U. C. in arch, turns to Strange Man in doorway. He has followed her and is now at her L. Blanche has arranged her hood about her face and smiles.

BLANCHE.   Whoever you are—I have always depended on the kindness of strangers.

She takes Strange Man's downstage arm, and they start through living room. Woman, following, picks up her bag from the bed. Pablo faces upstage. In living room, Stanley has resumed his place, and on above line, Steve sits down in his place, below table. Blanche and Strange Man go to front door. Stella turns as Blanche approaches. "Varsouviana" music rises.

STELLA.   Blanche! Blanche! Blanche!

Blanche ignores her sister and starts around into street above, Man coming to her upstage side, Blanche taking his arm. Woman follows, and when they pass the spiral, Eunice hands Woman Blanche's bag, then steps a bit R., looking after the little procession. Stanley rises, comes to L. of Stella, on steps, takes her in his arms. Pablo returns to table, sits.

STANLEY.   Stella?

Stella sobs with inhuman abandon. There is something luxurious in her complete surrender to crying now that her sister is gone. Stanley speaks to her voluptuously.

Now, honey. Now, love. Now, now, love. Now, now, love. Now, love…

Music approaches a crescendo. The little procession passes across through street toward U. L. exit.

STEVE.   *(As curtain starts to fall.)* All right, boys—this game is seven-card stud.

He deals cards.

THE CURTAIN COMES DOWN SLOWLY

END OF PLAY

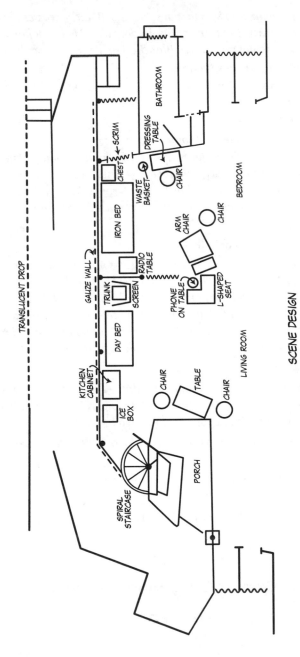

SCENE DESIGN

"A STREETCAR NAMED DESIRE"

DESIGN BY
JO MIELZINER

PROPERTY LIST
(Use this space to create props lists for your production)

SOUND EFFECTS
(Use this space to create sound effects lists for your production)

Dear reader,

Thank you for supporting playwrights by purchasing this acting edition! You may not know that Dramatists Play Service was founded, in 1936, by the Dramatists Guild and a number of prominent play agents to protect the rights and interests of play-wrights. To this day, we are still a small company committed to our partnership with the Guild, and by proxy all playwrights, established and aspiring, working in the English language.

Because of our status as a small, independent publisher, we respect-fully reiterate that this text may not be distributed or copied in any way, or uploaded to any file-sharing sites, including ones you might think are private. Photocopying or electronically distributing books means both DPS and the playwright are not paid for the work, and that ultimately hurts playwrights everywhere, as our profits are shared with the Guild.

We also hope you want to perform this play! Plays are wonderful to read, but even better when seen. If you are interested in performing or producing the play, please be aware that performance rights must be obtained through Dramatists Play Service. This is true for *any* public performance, even if no one is getting paid or admission is not being charged. Again, playwrights often make their sole living from performance royalties, so performing plays without paying the royalty is ultimately a loss for a real writer.

This acting edition is the **only approved text for performance.** There may be other editions of the play available for sale from other publishers, but DPS has worked closely with the playwright to ensure this published text reflects their desired text of all future productions. If you have purchased a revised edition (sometimes referred to as other types of editions, like "Broadway Edition," or "[Year] Edition"), that is the only edition you may use for perfor-mance, unless explicitly stated in writing by Dramatists Play Service.

Finally, this script cannot be changed without written permission from Dramatists Play Service. If a production intends to change the script in any way—including casting against the writer's intentions for characters, removing or changing "bad" words, or making other cuts however small—without permission, they are breaking the law. And, perhaps more importantly, changing an artist's work. Please don't do that!

We are thrilled that this play has made it into your hands. We hope you love it as much as we do, and thank you for helping us keep the American theater alive and vital.

Note on Songs/Recordings, Images, or Other Production Design Elements

Be advised that Dramatists Play Service, Inc., neither holds the rights to nor grants permission to use any songs, recordings, images, or other design elements mentioned in the play. It is the responsibility of the producing theater/organization to obtain permission of the copyright owner(s) for any such use. Additional royalty fees may apply for the right to use copyrighted materials.

For any songs/recordings, images, or other design elements mentioned in the play, works in the public domain may be substituted. It is the producing theater/organization's responsibility to ensure the substituted work is indeed in the public domain. Dramatists Play Service, Inc., cannot advise as to whether or not a song/arrangement/recording, image, or other design element is in the public domain.

NOTES
(Use this space to make notes for your production)

NOTES
(Use this space to make notes for your production)

NOTES
(Use this space to make notes for your production)

NOTES
(Use this space to make notes for your production)

NOTES
(Use this space to make notes for your production)